A Man and a Motorcycle

This book was made possible in part by the Stichting Democratie en Media (Foundation for Democracy and Media), Fonds Pascal Decroos voor Bijzondere Journalistiek (Pascal Decroos Fund for Investigative Journalism) and the V-fonds (National Fund for Freedom and Veterans Affairs). Afghanistan Analysts Network co-funded the translation. Publishing house The First Draft Press of Alex Strick van Linschoten and Felix Kuehn also contributed to the translation.

A Man and
a Motorcycle

How Hamid Karzai
Became Afghanistan's President

Bette Dam

Ipso Facto Publishers

Ipso Facto Publishers
www.if-publishers.com

Dam, Bette – 1979 –

A Man and a Motorcycle, How Hamid Karzai came to Power.

ISBN: 9789077386132

Ipso Facto Publishers are available for special promotions and premiums. For details contact Director Jan Banning.
info@janbanning.com

First English Edition August 2014

This book was published in Dutch in August 2009, with De Arbeiderspers Amsterdam

Cover designed by Andrei Bat
Cover photo by Ruben Terlou
Formatting by Paul Salvette

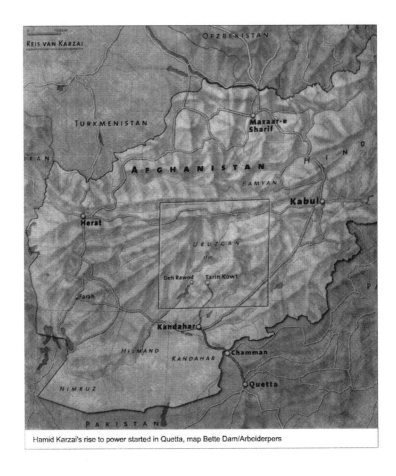

Hamid Karzai's rise to power started in Quetta, map Bette Dam/Arbeiderpers

Contents

Key Characters

JAN MOHAMMED (Popolzai): Karzai's principal ally in Uruzgan. The Taliban imprisoned him in 2000 when they learned that he and Karzai were planning to revolt. Karzai depended heavily on Jan Mohammed's network when he began the uprising after 9/11.

AHMAD WALI KARZAI (Popolzai): Karzai's half-brother and the "logistics man" of the uprising. Through the CIA, he provides him with food, money and satellite telephones.

SAID RAHIM (Popolzai): Karzai's messenger. A young man who hardly knew what was going on, and who was constantly sent out to recruit supporters for Karzai.

MOHAMMED SHAH (Popolzai): Karzai's head security guard who was sent into the South of Afghanistan after Said to prepare for Karzai's arrival.

HAJI MUND (Popolzai): Karzai's second security guard, assigned to protect him during the trip from Pakistan to Uruzgan.

HAJI FAIZULLAH (Popolzai): Karzai's third security guard, also assigned to protect him during the trip from Pakistan to Uruzgan.

AHMED KARZAI (Popolzai): took Karzai (his Uncle) across the border on the motorcycle.

ABDUL RAHIM AKHUNDZADA (Popolzai): taught the Taliban. His home was the first safe house that Hamid Karzai planned to use in Tarin Kot.

ABDUL GHANI MAMA ("The Rich Uncle", Popolzai): A stalwart supporter of Jan Mohammed. He was also recruited by the messenger Said. His was the second address in Tarin Kot where Karzai planned to hide.

ABDUL AZIZ SAHIBZADA (or Aziz Agha Pir Jan, Alikozai): before the Taliban rule he was the Uruzgan police chief under Jan Mohammed. He supported Karzai and was outraged when it looked like Karzai might not become president.

MUALIM RAHMATULLAH (Popolzai): one of the major Popolzai in Tarin Kot while Jan Mohammed was in prison, but he hesitated when called on by Karzai.

ROZI KHAN: a leading elder of the Barakzai in Uruzgan whose tribe members tried to kill Karzai in the nineties but in 2001 Rozi Khan opted for Karzai's revolt.

HASHEM KHAN (Ghilzai) Karzai's ticket to rival tribes in Uruzgan, which he would otherwise have trouble approaching, being Popolzai.

IBRAHIM AKHUNDZADA (Popolzai): provided Karzai with a second name in Deh Rawud, even though he considered Karzai's action to be suicidal. His connections with the Taliban were crucial for the revolt's success.

MULLAH NAQIBULLAH (Alikozai): surrendered to the Taliban in 1994 (but didn't become a member). After 9/11 he switched sides and negotiated with the Taliban on behalf of Karzai.

GUL AGHA SHERZAI (Barakzai): from Kandahar. Was governor of Kandahar province before the Taliban took control. He worked with Karzai during the Taliban regime, but after 9/11 he went his own way.

MULLAH MOHAMMAD OMAR (Hotak [Ghilzai]): Spent his youth in Uruzgan. Was the head of the Taliban regime and remains leader of the movement.

MULLAH ABDUL GHANI BARADAR (Popalzai) from Deh Rawud, and an important Taliban commander.

MULLAH SHAFIQ (Kakar): from the Mirabad Valley in Uruzgan and an important Taliban leader in Uruzgan. Above all an adversary of Jan Mohammed.

'GRAIG' (American): a CIA agent and Karzai's supporter in the uprising.

JASON AMERINE (American): US Army captain leading the Special Forces A-team that eventually helped Karzai in Uruzgan.

JAMES DOBBINS (American): Special Representative of US President George W. Bush for the Afghan Opposition. He attempted to form a new Afghan administration.

ABDUL SATTAR SIRAT (Uzbek): tried to prevent Karzai's appointment as president at the United Nations conference in Bonn, Germany.

Sources

This book is based on more than 150 interviews conducted between the autumn of 2007 and the winter of 2008 with Afghan, American, Pakistani and European participants described in the events. In 2013 and 2014, the author interviewed some participants again and updated the book accordingly. Many of the interviews were conducted entirely or partially on the record. Others were held under ground rules designed to protect the identity of the source interviewed. The material presented attempts to connect background interviews with open source material such as declassified documents and work published by journalists and scholars. Since not much is written about what actually happened in southern Afghanistan in 2001, interviews with witnesses were crucial.

Prologue

WHEN I MET the Afghan president for the first time, he nonchalantly accepted the small gift I'd brought for him. It was March 2008, a month after the deadliest suicide attack in Afghanistan in which 100 people were killed, and a week or two before Karzai would escape death at a military parade when gunmen started shooting at him.

My present was a *patu*, a shawl for men of the type often worn in the south of the country. "Nice, nice," he said tepidly. Karzai was preoccupied. It was eight thirty in the morning and he had just arrived in his black armoured car with security vehicles ahead and behind him. He had just been to the doctor. When the car door was opened, the security guards looked around apprehensively, anxious to get the president safely across the last few yards and into the palace. "Eh? The doctor? Oh, just a routine checkup," said the president, laughing aside my question.

Four or five clerics and assistants surrounded Karzai in the palace hall, all with different requests. They were dressed in slightly oversized dark suits, their hair shiny with gel. Karzai was the only one wearing a traditional long shirt with wide cotton pants. He addressed them: "What do you want? And you? And you?" He signed something, briefly held a telephone to his ear and gave instructions to his chief of protocol.

I had been given twenty minutes during breakfast to talk about his revolt in 2001 and how he managed to become the president of Afghanistan. If this kept up, it would be a very short interview. Karzai was far too busy with the present-day Afghanistan.

I was grateful to get any time in his schedule at all. It had taken me seven months just to get in the palace door. At first I couldn't even get an interview with Karzai's spokesperson. Then I made it as far as the waiting room, but I was told that I had to leave. After a few quiet months, a bomb had exploded in the north. It was a bloodbath; several politicians and children were killed. The Taliban had not claimed responsibility for the attack. It was chaos. "Karzai will answer your questions on paper," the frazzled spokesperson had said, and walked away. After that, Karzai was travelling a lot outside the country.

After much perseverance, I finally got an appointment with the spokesperson's deputy. His English was poor; he was more in charge of the Afghan media. I asked him if he could let Karzai know about all the people I had talked to. I mentioned names of men from Kandahar and Uruzgan I had already interviewed about his journey in 2001. They had helped Karzai to become president, I pointed out. Surely the protagonist couldn't be left out? The spokesman's deputy didn't understand and barely looked at me, but apparently the fact I knew all of Karzai's close friends impressed him. "Return to your hotel, we'll call you," he said. Two days later I received a phone call: "We have discussed it with His Excellency and he wants to meet you." A day later everything was arranged. I was told: "The president has twenty minutes. Make sure you are here an hour and a half early because the security check is a long process."

The presidential palace is located in the heart of Kabul, far from the enemy. My translator took me there in a small Toyota Corolla. We drove at a snail's pace past the busy bazaar with its large carts piled high with fruit and nuts, past the mosque with the blue dome that was still unfinished because the owner had been killed, past women in filthy *burqas* who tapped aggressively on the windshield, begging for money. Slowly we approached a high wall and a checkpoint cocooned in stacks of sandbags, with the barrels of Kalashnikovs sticking out. These walls contained not only Karzai, but also the offices of the CIA, the United Nations, and American diplomats. Our little car joined the line of SUVs with bulky bodyguards protecting the officials in their backseats. The large armoured jeeps drive through the city without stopping. The jammers on the car roofs ensure that no phone calls can be made, because any telephone call could potentially detonate a bomb.

The palace security guard looked taken aback—our car didn't exactly fit in. "Bettie Dom," my translator told the man. Curious, he pressed his face against the back window. "Ooh, blue eyes!" he exclaimed once he saw me. His superior gave the go-ahead, and we drove on. I was announced via walkie-talkie and so we rolled slowly on, from one security check to another, until we were inside.

At the last checkpoint the atmosphere was tense. We

were close to the palace now and I had to walk the rest of the way. "Can't I come with you?" the translator whispered. But Karzai spoke English and I chose to go alone. My bag and pens were taken from me, and I only managed to hold on to my tape recorder. One of the security guards unexpectedly said, "Tea?" I smiled. A small hint of Afghan hospitality after all.

Our first meeting was to take place in the great hall of Karzai's presidential palace. The building was called 'House of the Flowers'. It was quiet; the only audible sound was the clicking of staff member's shoes along the marble floor. Security guards moved like shadows through the building. While I waited I stood near the long, broad staircase with the chandeliers suspended above it. A worn red carpet ran from the top of the stairs down to just outside the main entrance, where two stiff Buckingham Palace-type guards briefly salute passing visitors. These stairs knew how brutal life could be here in Kabul. Afghanistan's bloody saga, its countless wars between leaders, had been written here too. In 1978 Afghan communists shot the country's then-president, Daoud Khan, and members of his family, right here in the middle of the palace. The bodies collapsed on the marble stairs where the red carpet now lies. The murders were the prologue to the Soviet occupation a year later, which hurled Afghanistan into a war that didn't leave much of the country standing. After the Soviets left and the Afghans fought one another, the palace was regularly besieged. The communist president Najibullah couldn't make it out on time. In 1996, when the Taliban seized control, they managed to capture him. Tied to the back of a car, they dragged him through the city, tortured and castrated him and then shot him dead before hanging him from a traffic police post near the entrance to the palace. His body remained there for days. His head had snapped forward after the rope had broken his neck. The traffic police post is still standing, right by the CIA compound and Karzai's presidential palace.

When Karzai had finished his morning appointments, he invited me into the spacious meeting room. It was neatly whitewashed and the ceiling ornamented. The palace restoration was coming along nicely. Outside, plasterers and bricklayers were hard at work erasing the scars of history. We sat down at the end of a long, narrow table surrounded by some thirty chairs. Only the corner at the far end was neatly set for two.

"So, Uruzgan," said the president. I nodded. For a moment it seemed odd that I, a Westerner, wanted to write "his" story. Who was I to presume that I could comprehend this society? I explained that I wanted to describe his uprising in 2001, based on as many eyewitness accounts as possible. Again I mentioned the names of the men I had already interviewed. The president leaned toward me eagerly: "What? Really? You spoke to all those people?" For a brief moment the tight schedule and the stress seemed to fall away from Karzai. The security guard standing behind us, dressed in black, stirred slightly. He seemed to think any suspicious movement could be an assassination attempt. "You know," the president said, "no one has ever done this." I've definitely got his attention. "But wait, let's have breakfast. We'll have some bread with honey—

whatever you wish. A croissant, *naan*, we have everything."
He gestured invitingly to the table with the porcelain
settings. "What do you want, ma'am—coffee, tea?" and he
nodded to the servant who has joined the security guard.
"We used the kind of shawl you gave me in Uruzgan as
well," he exclaimed, delighted. "And you know," he
continues eagerly, "I still have a coat from that period. Yes,
indeed. I still have that coat. I really didn't have enough
clothes with me, Bette, I really didn't. Oh, it was so cold
there at that time. Then the Americans gave me that coat."
His mind went back to his own revolt, and it obviously
evoked feelings of euphoria. "My men were there, men I
had known for so long!" They were heroes to Karzai, heroes
who accompanied him in during the uprising "Uruzgan
was the centre of my resistance, Bette. Truly."

"Call Qader Haideri," Karzai suddenly bellowed across
the hall. The spokesman rushed off. I know Qader. I tried
to explain to Karzai that I'd already interviewed him.
Besides, I wanted Karzai all to myself, and I didn't have
much time. But he wouldn't hear of it. Qader is one of
those men from Karzai's uprising, originally from the
remote town of Deh Rawud in western Uruzgan province.
After Karzai took power, he brought him along to the
palace. "Qader is now head of, eh, what do you call it? The
Tenth Department," the president explained. The Tenth
Department was one of the departments of the Afghan
secret service (NDS) responsible for the security of foreign
delegations, their offices, and other locations where many
Westerners live, like the deluxe Serena Hotel in Kabul.
Qaider's office was located in the vicinity of the presidential

palace and so he showed up in no time at our breakfast table. "Look," cried Karzai, "this is Bette and she's researching our mission!" I nodded at Qader and he nodded back. The man didn't speak a word of English, had a busy job, but out of respect he stayed for the conversation. "Bette, this is the general. He's my very best friend, really. When someone has embraced your struggle and you win, they have the right to be rewarded," said Karzai proudly. "That's how it works here. Oh, and do you know Haji Hafizullah? How delightful! You must meet him as well," the president exclaimed energetically. "He was with me on the motorcycle when we crossed the border. Now he is working at the Afghan embassy in the United Arab Emirates." Apparently the president realised that I was aware that Hafizullah was just a simple security guard in 2001. "Yes, he was my bodyguard, but he studied economics before that. Now he's first or second secretary in Abu Dhabi, at our embassy... Why wasn't I told sooner that Bette was in the country?" he exclaimed, addressing the spokesman, who looked disturbed. I could imagine what he was thinking: will we ever get to that next appointment? Breakfast was running late already. But Karzai ignored him. "How long are you staying? Do you still have time? Do you know Mohammed Shah?" I nod. He was a questionable character who allegedly dealt in drugs. "Shah is at Kandahar Airport as we speak and he's on his way here. You're lucky—two weeks ago I appointed him head of security of my residence.".

We subsequently went through the long list of his heroes of 2001 who now have – qualified or not—received key positions in his government. People from Helmand and Kandahar, but also from other parts of the country: those who helped Karzai take power and who he would never forget. "They were the centre of my resistance," the president murmured again. He said he hardly remembered the Americans who later supported him. "Captain Jason Amerine?" Only in a later interview would he recall him. "Yes, that's right, he joined later."

The same happened when I asked Karzai about controversial assistance from the CIA. Immediately he denied their presence. But after my trips to Uruzgan, and after long talks with his men there, it wasn't possible for Karzai to change the reality of what had happened. The men there told me about the involvement of the CIA in Karzai's mission. Later, when Karzai agreed to another long interview, I asked him, 'do you know Graig'? Karzai's face spoke for itself. For a second I could see concern, realising he couldn't hide the role of the CIA any more. Then Karzai his mood turned instantly, and he became enthusiastic, saying: "Graig, Graig, he is my best friend! How do you know him?" Raptured, he lost control over his words, not taking into account any sensitivity about the delicate issue. He started telling me more about their relationship, giving away all he tried to hide earlier. At the time of my research and interviews with the president – 2008 and 2009 – Graig Vogel was the head of the CIA in Afghanistan and known to be very good friends with Karzai, visiting his office regularly. Karzai suddenly stood up, and offered the most unexpected: do you want a picture of us together in Tarin Kowt, of Graig and me? I said, yes, of course.

Karzai offered me a flight to Uruzgan. "You have to see it either way—you must see how beautiful it is." He pushed it as if he was talking about a vacation paradise. "Beautiful orchards, hospitality, and delicious yoghurt." Eight years on, he still had mostly romantic associations with the now very turbulent region. Uruzgan represented success for him, that much was obvious.

I had a multitude of choices for transport to Uruzgan. Do I take the viceroy Jan Mohammed's helicopter? Do I ride with a convoy of Jan Mohammed's close family member Matiullah, who also helped in 2001, who was one of Karzai's allies, and who now – due to the NATO convoys—had become a millionaire by securing the road between Tarin Kot and Kandahar city? Or do I take a trip with the senator, a tribesman of Karzai who helped him also in 2001 – and in return – was now representing Uruzgan province in the Senate in Kabul? In the end I chose to go to Tarin Kot by myself, staying for a week with Aziz, another of the men who supported Karzai in 2001. He wouldn't be present himself; he was away, undergoing heart surgery in India, paid for by Karzai.

It turned out later that Karzai knew exactly where I was staying. It was characteristic of the president that he still kept up with "his" Afghans: if they belonged to Karzai's group, they would of course be in touch with him. They were lifelong bonds. He knew their travel schedules, when they would be in town and what their plans would be. When writing about Karzai as a leader, it often occurred to me that he saw Afghanistan as being only these men, and not much more. This book will show how the group Karzai relied on enriched themselves through patronage and nepotism over the years, making governors billionaires, and police commanders dictators, a trend that would show what corruption meant in his government, and how insurgency is created by pushing more and more excluded groups into the opposition. Karzai's men are seldom seen at his presidential desk, but they often drop by his private house. In these evenings, they discuss their business and tribal wheeling and dealing, hunkered down around huge plates of rice and lamb. This is how Afghan politics work. This kind of informal loyalty of tribes and families determines the course of Afghan politics.

ONE

Back to 2001: The Message

"**H**AVE SAID COME here," Karzai instructed one of his doormen. It had been less than two weeks since 9/11 and Karzai wanted to see the young man immediately. Said, from a hamlet in Uruzgan, had been in the city for several days already, and now his leader needed him. The rather awkward young Afghan walked along the dirty, busy streets of Quetta, the Pakistani border city and capital of Baluchistan province. Official counts estimate roughly half a million residents, although the number could be quite a bit higher. In recent decades Quetta has practically turned into an Afghan city, a safe haven for people who no longer feel secure in their home country. The presence of Afghan drug traffickers, businessmen, elders, and vast refugee camps—it all stems from the thirty years of war in Afghanistan. It was the last week of September 2001, and Said walked calmly amid all the activity, past the rickshaws, crowded market stalls, and heaps of blackmarket electronic equipment.[1]

The elongated *kota* (guest room) in Karzai's mud brick mansion on the outskirts of Quetta was crowded. Said frowned. "What's going on here?" he asked himself.

Security had suddenly been heightened at the luxurious residence. The master of the house, fearing betrayal, had given surprisingly strict instructions to the three security guards at the entrance. In this manicured Quetta suburb, home to many well-to-do Afghans, Karzai received one person after another. Afghans, diplomats, journalists, all recently arrived. They came with one question on their minds: What's going to happen? Like Karzai, many of the Afghans were exiles in Pakistan who'd fled the Taliban. Televisions were turned on all over town. They anxiously followed the news about their country. Some were sensitive to the fact that Afghanistan had disappeared from the front pages of the international papers quite some time ago. Now, however, the country was in the spotlight, and everyone wanted to know what the US would do next. The Afghans were all seated on the floor along the high wall of the long room, their backs straight and their bare feet tucked under them. Some murmured amongst themselves in small groups, others talked loudly, frequently interrupting one another.

Said, who had travelled all the way from Tarin Kot, the small capital of Uruzgan province a couple of days earlier, paid little attention to the heated discussions about Afghanistan's future. He had missed the news about September 11th because televisions were banned in Afghanistan and nobody had told him about it during his travels to Quetta. But the devoted servant knew one thing: Karzai wished to see him as soon as possible and he should hurry up. A doorman led Said across the *kota* directly to Karzai's private quarters. He quickly shook a few hands on the way. Some men stood, out of politeness, to grab Said's hands and asked him all manner of questions. It was a short moment of friendliness, despite the fact that they were all strangers. A brief embrace or even a kiss was exchanged. Said asked how they were doing, and how their families were doing, but he didn't go through the whole elaborate greeting ritual. In one corner of the room, on a coffee table, a television repeatedly showed images of the collapsing skyscrapers. The talking heads on the screen moved their mouths rapidly. The collapse of the buildings was filmed from several different angles: the camera followed the enormous dust cloud in Manhattan and then turned to the wide-angle shot of panicked citizens screaming while they ran. The images meant nothing to Said.

Karzai calmly greeted him with a *"Salam aleikum"* (peace be with you). *"wa Aleikum Salam"* (and peace be with you), the young man answered obligingly as he respectfully bowed his head to his elder. For several years, Karzai had been sporting a trim salt-and-pepper beard and he'd dressed—as always—in the traditional *shalwar kameez*, a shirt down to his knees over roomy cotton pants, tightened around the waist with a drawstring. He rarely wore the turban prescribed by the Taliban. On occasion Karzai covered his head with a small white skull cap, of the kind often used as a base for the turban. He had inherited it from his murdered father. The desk was covered with telephones, papers, and lists of names. The warm words of welcome were repeated according to Afghan custom: "How are you? Did you arrive safely? How are your brothers and your family?" They briefly clasped each other's hands, bound in the ancient tradition—the poor young man from remote Uruzgan province and the affluent, English-speaking Hamid Karzai. They looked somewhat alike. They were roughly the same height although Said had a dark, fist-long beard, as enforced by the Taliban. They answered each other's questions a few times with "Thank God, thank God, and be safe." After the lengthy greeting, Karzai told Said what to do, without disclosing the full plan, which would be too dangerous. Go back to Uruzgan, Karzai said: "You must go back to your province and deliver a message." Without any knowledge of the purpose of his trip, Said would have to visit several villages and cities to invite a small group of eight or nine Afghans whom Karzai wanted to see in Quetta as soon as possible.

Said had to go from door to door, passing his message on in person in the same way that messengers had done in biblical times.[2] There were no mobile phones in Taliban territory and the landlines weren't very reliable either. International aid workers used satellite telephones every now and then to fill the gap, but the Taliban tried to root them out. Telephones were often stolen from their offices. Sometimes it was a simple matter of theft, but more often it was done because the Taliban didn't trust the aid workers and suspected them of espionage. In general only small, limited-range walkie-talkies were used in Afghanistan. In this case Karzai relied on Said, not only because he trusted him, but because the people receiving the message would know where they stood with him. Afghans don't open up if they don't trust the knock on the door. Therefore, in order to eliminate all doubt, a relative is often sent. Others prefer to use an imam or an apprentice imam to make sure messages are delivered. Karzai chose to use Said, the small entrepreneur from a village near Uruzgan's capital Tarin Kot, not only because he was a member of Karzai's own tribe, but also because he was from the same tribe as the families to whom he would be delivering messages. A few of the men were even directly related to him.

Said returned to Uruzgan in a taxi paid for by Karzai. At the border crossing near Chaman he merged onto the long, straight road to Kandahar, the biggest city in southern Afghanistan and birthplace of the Taliban. The taxi flew by mud brick villages that blended in with the flat steppe landscape surrounding Kandahar city. Traffic rushed along on this centuries-old trade route to India, Iran, and to the "'Stans", the former Soviet republics such as Kazakhstan or Turkmenistan. Kandahar city lies at the heart of this route where merchandise, contraband, and carloads of families would all be on their way to far-off destinations. Large trucks with hand-painted advertise-ments on their sides and cabins festooned with ringing bells—the so-called 'jingle trucks'—changed lanes without warning. Motorcycles swerved around the cars and trucks, their drivers bent low over the handlebars. Men on bicycle carts loaded with brushwood thinking only of the cold winter ahead. In this ancient landscape with its backdrop of jagged mountains, everyone heads for Kandahar city, once taken by Alexander the Great's armies, about 300 years BCE. He was followed by various ethnic groups who struggled for dominance in this mountainous country at the end of the Himalayas. Chinese, Arabs, Mongols,

Uzbeks, and Persians fought over the region for hundreds of years. The Pashtuns rose to prominence from the eighteenth century, and it was they who formally established the land of the Afghans—Afghanistan. The small groups of steadily walking nomads Said viewed from the taxi—slender outlines moving across the level landscape—didn't seem to be paying much attention to the passage of time. Dressed in long, beige garments and long head-scarves, they continued stoically on their journey with their sheep and barking dogs, gradually disappearing in the fog of desert dust.

Kandahar was still firmly under the control of the Taliban, the fundamentalist Muslim government that ruled large parts of Afghanistan, and whose authority had been unchallenged since 1994, especially in the south. Although Kabul was the official capital of Afghanistan for years, the Taliban ruled the country from Kandahar city. This is where the elusive Taliban leader, Mullah Omar, had his office, where he kept numerous walkie-talkies on hand to stay in touch with his commanders in the field. The Taliban come from the lap of the Pashtun. This proud people, some 13 million strong, live mainly in southern Afghanistan, with an additional 25 million living across the border in Pakistan. The Pashtuns on both sides are strongly connected. The border between Afghanistan and Pakistan – the Durand Line – was drawn by the British in the nineteenth century and isn't recognised by most Pashtuns. To this day, some Pashtuns would rather reunite in a sovereign Pashtunistan.

The Pashtun are divided into a web of hundreds of

tribes, sub-tribes and large families and clans. These tribal people, who make up a substantial part of the Afghan population, are very critical of the central government. For decades the leaders of Afghanistan came from among the Pashtun, but those kings and presidents barely managed to govern their own people. The clans or sub-tribes of the Pashtun are their strongest competition. They often have their own little fiefdoms and are accustomed to handling their own affairs. They defend their families and their land, to the death if need be. Relations between these fiefdoms often form a tangle of temporary alliances and feuds that outsiders have a hard time comprehending. Feuds between families regularly result in murder, and cycles of revenge can go on for generations. Memories, especially of violence, are long, and so conflicts can lie dormant, only to suddenly reerupt years later.

Foreign military forces also ran aground on this for them difficult social structure. A former Taliban leader once said that foreign powers have always found it easy to enter Afghanistan. "But how do you leave this morass of tribes?" he mused.[3] Once on the ground, troops would quickly become bogged down in local struggles. Even the Taliban suffered from this phenomenon, often exploited by crafty elders when they wished to rid themselves of a rival. Knowledge of shifting allegiances is crucial to survival. Pashtun leaders have an almost full-time job keeping up with changes in influential family networks. Even if they don't have telephones or television, they know exactly who's who, where loyalties lie, and where betrayal lurks.

After traversing the flat desert region around Kandahar

city, Said went north, high into the mountains. His destination—Uruzgan—was where he would find Karzai's strongest allies. Some say the region was dubbed "like a day" in the 1960's due to its altitude: so close to the sun that it never gets dark. In the past there were no provinces in southern Afghanistan and the whole area was governed by elders under the name Loy Kandahar (Greater Kandahar). In the 1960s the central government in Kabul decided to form provinces in order to break the elders' power. Whether it has helped is doubtful. Politics in Uruzgan is still tribally and economically oriented toward Kandahar. Even today the elders, not the central government in Kabul, usually determine what needs to be done in this small province in south-central Afghanistan.

When Said arrived in Tarin Kot in the last days of September 2001, it was business as usual. In the bazaar men in pastel-coloured shirts stood around the many stalls. Others sat hunkered down for hours by the roadside, working through the latest local gossip. Most men wore the Taliban-prescribed turbans. Black and white dominated, although this was more a matter of taste than of rule—other colours were permissible. Every now and then a pick-up truck with religious Taliban police in the back showed up on the dusty main street—otherwise everything seemed calm. The small *madrassas* (religious schools) were full of boys, also wearing the prescribed turbans. They studied the Koran; math, geography, and other subjects disappeared with the arrival of the Taliban. In the afternoons the students worked to make money for their families. One joined the tailor; another would help out at the market.

Uruzgan is one of Afghanistan's poorest and least developed provinces. People here have hardly any education, and they live mainly by the morals and values set by their elder. They are conservative and violent, even by Afghan standards. In Kabul people always shake their heads contemptuously at mention of the area. For those city-dwellers, this is a remote, backward, and insignificant corner of their country.

Said didn't need to be in the capital Tarin Kot. He instructed the taxi to follow the river north, to Kot Wal village, where he would find the first address Karzai had given him. The taxi drove across sandy tracks full of potholes to the *kala* he needed, a typical Afghan house with sand-coloured walls at least eight feet high. From the outside Said could see nothing. All homes are hidden behind these walls. Every patriarch can choose for himself how high a wall he puts around his household. This is how he protects his family and especially the women from peeping toms, thieves, and other threats to his honour.

Here, as in all of southern Afghanistan, people live by the unwritten tribal codes of the *Pashtunwali*, the Rules of Honour.[4] While *badal* (revenge) is mainly a way to defend one's honour, *melmastia* (hospitality) is a means of improving it. The status of the family patriarch is measured by the number of people who visit him. It's no coincidence, therefore, that the most important part of the *kala* is the *kota*, as they call the guest room. It's the back room of Pashtun politics. This is where the family patriarch holds court. The guests can be people dropping by for their pay, for advice on family disputes, to collect debts, to do business, or travellers seeking a place to stay for shorter or longer periods. So the guest quarters are the governing centres of tribal society, as it were. For this reason the Pashtun first builds the *kota* before he builds the other quarters. In the *kota* the host can show what he's worth as deputy mayor of his tribe or clan.

Said knew the way unerringly in Kot Wal. Abdul Ghani Mama, the man he needed to summon for Karzai, was his uncle. He was ushered cordially inside the *kota*, and explained the reason for his visit. The host wasn't surprised. It was not the first time Karzai had asked his Uruzgan connections, through Said, to come to Quetta. In the past few years Karzai's *kota* had functioned exactly like the guest rooms in Uruzgan. Said himself went to see Karzai on a few occasions as well. Local Taliban officials or his local rivals had stolen his crop. A few times he had arrived at his field in the mornings only to find it empty. The honour code of his people demanded he take action immediately. Since Said was only a simple farmer, he could hardly handle the dispute. He sought support from Karzai, who helped him, even covering his travel expenses to and from Quetta. And Said was returning the favour by serving as Karzai's messenger.

After thinking about the invitation, Abdul Ghani Mama decided to accept. He knew Karzai mainly through his own father, whom he viewed as a respected leader. It was, however, risky. Despite the *kalas'* high walls, little remains secret. Neighbours and relatives keep a sharp eye on one another. A prolonged absence would be noticed immediately, leading to questions about the absentee's whereabouts.

None of the invitees wanted their visit with Karzai in Quetta to become public knowledge because of Karzai's reputation as anti-Taliban.

In the end, Said persuaded Abdul Ghani Mama and seven other tribesmen. Most of them chose to travel in the evening so they could hear what Karzai had to say and then quickly return to their families.

TWO

9/11: New Opportunities

ON SEPTEMBER 11, 2001, Hamid Karzai was in the Pakistani capital, Islamabad. He had just been to the U.S. Embassy when he received a phone call from his half-brother, Ahmad Wali, who lived with him in Quetta since leaving the United States. He told Karzai what he had just witnessed on television: an aircraft had crashed into the World Trade Center in New York City.

Karzai had a strange sense of foreboding when he hung up, although he continued on his evening walk. He was on his way to the mosque. When his half-brother called again, he slowed his pace for a moment. The news of the second aircraft and further hijackings was a blow. "This is al-Qaeda. This is an attack on America," Karzai exclaimed. For a while both men spoke only in superlatives. "Am I imagining this?" asked Ahmad Wali. "I warned them about this so often," said Karzai. "How on earth can this have happened to the Americans, who have so much intelligence?" Ahmad Wali asked again. Both men were sure that this would be the end of the Taliban—the Americans wouldn't take the attack lying down. Karzai heard his brother shout at his security guards. "The Taliban are finished," he bellowed exuberantly. The brothers were aware that something big was about to happen in Afghanistan. "Now we can stand up to the Taliban. Now we have something powerful behind us."

The following day Karzai flew back to Quetta. He had arranged to go to Peshawar, another large Pakistani border town that had become home to many Afghans, but he cancelled and went to his house. Several of his compatriots had already gathered there, eager to hear the latest news from Karzai. They knew Karzai was not only familiar with Afghan politics, but was also well-informed about the developments in the West.

During the course of the next few days things got busier in Karzai's *kota*. Not only Afghans, but foreign diplomats, CIA, Brits, and Western journalists dropped by. They all wanted to know what the consequences of the attacks would be for Afghanistan. Karzai cordially received his guests and patiently gave interviews. "I warned the Americans about this," he said to one of the journalists. "If they had taken action sooner, lots of American mothers and children wouldn't have lost loved ones." At the same time he pointed out the fate of his own people, who had suffered under the Taliban in recent years. "Afghans are a poor people," he told them. "No one paid attention to us."

Journalists observed Afghan elders coming and going, from Karzai's and other Afghans' homes, to hear the latest news. Also some Taliban-members Karzai had managed to stay in contact with, passed through looking to size up the situation. The men Said called upon in Uruzgan paid their respects as well. Said hadn't been able toconvince all the men Karzai had asked for. Some he hadn't even gone to see personally, passing Karzai's message via neighbouring tribal members. In the end, seven of those who had been invited made the perilous journey from Uruzgan to Quetta, among them an elderly imam who told his worshippers in the mosque his foot suddenly bothered him, and that he needed to see the famous doctor Wardak in Quetta.

Karzai told the seven men precisely what had happened in America and what it meant for their own country. They hadn't seen the images of collapsing towers and hijacked planes for themselves. "The Taliban are powerful in Uruzgan, but this will change now. I know it," said Karzai. "We are no longer alone—the West will support us," he repeated several times. "I have told you before that something will change, and the moment has come. A lot will happen and you must get involved." The Uruzganis listened intently to the well-groomed Karzai and their fingers glided through their fist-long beards. They appreciated the fact that Karzai could give a good speech, one of the skills expected of a good leader. A leader's voice must impress and command attention in full *kotas* and Karzai did just that. But they were sceptical. Karzai had given them lists of friends, kin, Taliban, ex-Taliban whom they must approach. What was he up to?

They had heard Karzai say it all before: that something would happen in the south.[5] That he would "go in" via Quetta, to stand up to the Taliban and slowly form his own militia, much like a warlord. He would mention connections with other strongmen who were also willing to do something about the Taliban. At that time he had also mentioned arranging American support. Someone in the group even remembered Karzai talking about an aircraft from the West that would end the Taliban regime with a few bombs. That was in 1998, shortly after al-Qaeda first announced itself by attacking two American embassies in Africa.

The idea of regime change definitely appealed to the Uruzganis in Karzai's *kota* in Quetta. Before the Taliban took control in 1994, they themselves had been in power, either as elders, police chiefs, or militia commanders. They would drive around in their staff cars, they had easy access to government funds, and they could hand out favours to their hearts' content in their *kotas*.

The Pashtuns had ruled Afghanistan for the most part, but not after the Soviets left in 1989. A Tajik, Burhanuddin Rabbani, came to power, but he barely held on. Powerful Pashtun warlords such as Gulbuddin Hekmatyar, founder of the conservative Hezb-e-Islami, strongly opposed the Northern Alliance that was made up of mainly Tajiks, Uzbeks, and Hazara that Rabbani relied upon for his power base. With help from Pakistan, Hekmatyar bombarded the Afghan capital with thousands of rockets. Afghanistan descended into a civil war—in those years everyone fought everyone and for all intents and purposes there was no longer any central government. Many Afghans look back at that period as a time when only dogs roamed the streets of Kabul.

In Uruzgan province Jan Mohammed rose to power in this chaos, after having played a vital role in the fight against the Soviets. Still, it wasn't a given that he would be governor. Jan Mohammed didn't belong to any of the major clans who had divided power among themselves prior to the Soviet invasion. Some Uruzganis claim he was a simple notary at the time.[6] Others are sure he made his living as a concierge. Whatever his origins, he was now an influential man, thanks to the rows of Kalashnikovs in his *kota*, taken from the Americans and the Soviets. In a defining moment, he had even held back from driving the Soviets out of Tarin Kot, because he preferred to continue stealing supplies and weapons from the weakened Red Army, if only so he could feed and reward his own warriors generously. Jan Mohammed's appointment as governor of Uruzgan gave rise to a lot of jealousy, in particular among the traditional leaders who came from renowned clans but who were marginalised after the Soviets left. They refused to address Jan Mohammed as *Khan*, the honorary title for an Afghan leader. Although he obviously realised his rapid rise to power in Uruzgan had mainly to do with his Kalashnikovs, rumour has it he was also supported by the Americans and Karzai's family.

Yet Jan Mohammed's influence in the early nineties was limited. In an attempt to gain more power and money, he wasn't quite able to establish effective control over all the tribes in the province. All the principal clans and sub-tribes retreated to their own fiefdoms, where they took little notice of the provincial government. Traveling across the region was challenging—every mile or so there would be a chain across the road to stop travellers for the purpose of extortion. Tribal strife broke out left and right and Jan Mohammed and his men joined in with a vengeance.

Several mysterious murders led to a longstanding feud between Jan Mohammed and members of the Barakzai, who form a large group in Uruzgan's capital, Tarin Kot. Among the many dead in the tribal rivalry was Jan Mohammed's brother, killed by an assassin. There were similar clashes in the city of Deh Rawud, where two large clans fought for control within a sub-tribe. A fight also broke out between two men of the Babozai tribe. A dispute over a rocket launcher caused the related elders Haji Hodud and Haji Hashem Khan to attack each other in Deh Rashan, north of Tarin Kot. And in far northern Uruzgan a bloody conflict developed between the Hazara and the Pashtun population.

A few hours away from Uruzgan in Kandahar, the group that would come to be known as 'the Taliban' were gathering in strength in 1994. The Taliban leaders owed their fame to two spectacular actions. They took control of a huge weapons depot in the town of Spin Boldak on the border with Pakistan, and later they were able to reopen the trade route running through Kandahar that had become virtually impassable due to checkpoints and road blocks. Elders from all the surrounding provinces travelled to Kandahar to find out who these newcomers were. What did they want? How strong were they? The police chief of Uruzgan province, Aziz Sahibzada, even drove to Kandahar city twice to size up the situation. He concluded that the Taliban were indeed becoming a significant force in and around Kandahar. For instance, the elder of his Alikozai tribe, Mullah Naqibullah, from northern Kandahar province, chose to side with the Taliban. Naqibullah was a military commander, yet he had handed over his arms and other equipment to the new rulers. On a later occasion, while on the road with Jan Mohammed to meet with the Karzai family in Quetta, Aziz saw the same pattern. Many had joined the Taliban, sometimes just by receiving bribes.

To his surprise, Aziz knew most of these new leaders. Many of them had lived in his province, but didn't belong to the governing clans or to the powerful tribes. "How could this happen?" Aziz asked himself, "These groups have no clout." Many Taliban came from tribes or families that were previously marginalised. This could be said of Mullah Omar, for instance, which is why Aziz didn't consider him a threat. After all, the man was a nomad, a *kuchi* from the insignificant Hotak tribe, Aziz said. He was a passer-by, an "import Uruzgani," not even born in Uruzgan, but in the neighbouring Kandahar province. When Omar's father died there, his mother remarried her husband's brother and they moved to Deh Rawud, to the west of Uruzgan. In Aziz's eyes, such a family meant nothing. Ask anyone, Aziz knew, which clan has the least land in Deh Rawud, and they will tell you that they do. Even in Deh Rawud there was some surprise about the rise of Omar, who added "Mullah" to his name later. That he was admired within his own tribe because he had lost an eye fighting against the Soviets wasn't terribly impressive. Aziz and other rulers at the time thought his eye could just as well have been damaged some other way.

Still, it would only take a few months before the Taliban were also in control in Uruzgan.[7] As in the rest of Afghanistan, after the war against the Soviets, it was no longer apparent who the real provincial rulers of Uruzgan were. The old elite had fled and the younger generation only knew violence. Even a servant could now be minister or president. One of them might get control with American support, another could be helped by the Pakistanis, and yet another might get a leg up from the Soviets.

Mullah Omar was certainly not the only Taliban to come from Uruzgan. The Taliban secretaries of health and justice and the Taliban governor of Kandahar all had ties to the area, as did several Taliban military commanders, like Mullah Dadullah, the commander who had lost a leg in battle against the Russians, and who since then often made appearances on horseback. He came from northwestern Char Chino district and he was one of the ten senior rulers of the Taliban. Jan Mohammed's nephew, Matiullah, had reportedly served under him. Dadullah's brother was also a renowned warrior from the area. The prominent Mullah Shafiq, from the same tribe as Mullah Omar and, according to some, a member of his clan, hailed from eastern Uruzgan and was considered one of the five major elders of Tarin Kot. Rumour in town had it that he had at least three Stinger shoulder-fired rocket launchers, gifts from the Americans, left over from the war against the Soviets. He and Jan Mohammed had been adversaries for years, and Shafiq chose the Taliban because at that point he felt marginalised by the former governor.

So it wasn't hard for the Taliban to take Uruzgan. Even Governor Jan Mohammed, having nowhere else to turn, supported them. The Karzai family had already urged him, through a messenger, to surrender. He gave "his animals and his rice and potato stores" to the Taliban and went home. Jan Mohammed's police chief Aziz did nothing to stop them either when they walked into his office. They took a gun, and the police cars. And when his young son tried to smuggle a lamp from the office, the Taliban stopped him in his tracks. "It's over for you, get out."

Initially the new rulers had been candid enough: they had a friendly approach and wanted reconciliation. In Uruzgan the change came about mainly through talking. In Tarin Kot they politely announced themselves through the central mosque's loudspeakers. There were also some meetings in the prayer house and most of the town's men had attended. "There will be peace," the Taliban announced. "Islam will triumph." Tribal contention, corruption, extortion, everything that was bringing the country down had to stop, they said. "We no longer want anything to do with self-serving warlords or elders. You must serve your country." Like Karzai would try later on in 2001, Taliban messengers were sent to their tribes and clans to announce the new era. Those talks were friendly and rather brief. Everything is going to be all right, the Taliban messengers promised. As far as anyone knows, no one died in the process. Two men from Tarin Kot resisted and fled. The Taliban quickly granted them amnesty.

THREE

A Diplomat Among Warlords

W HEN THE TALIBAN rose to power in 1994, Karzai
was at home in Quetta. Earlier that year he had
resigned as Deputy Minister of Foreign Affairs after a
dispute with President Rabbani and Mohammed Fahim
who was intelligence head, and now Hamid Karzai's vice
president. Karzai had been accused of insulting the regime
by contacting their enemy Hezb-e Islami, and was
subsequently interrogated. While he was in an interroga-
tion room in Kabul, where rockets still struck daily, a
projectile – accidentally or not—hit the building. He
escaped, slightly injured and reportedly managed to get to
Pakistan with the help of Gulbuddin Hekmatyar.[8] After
this run-in with Rabbani he returned to Quetta to live with
his father. He was in his late thirties then, but contrary to
Pashtun traditions he wasn't yet married or engaged. His
ministerial position had given him a diplomatic passport
that he used in the subsequent years to travel all around the
world.

Hamid Karzai – or Hamid Jan as many called him
then, a term of endearment for a sweet, likeable boy –
wasn't well-known at the time, but the American ambassa-

dor in Islamabad knew him to be well-informed.[9] He had quite a few Taliban representatives in his network. Mullah Ghaus, who would become the Taliban minister of foreign affairs, was a good friend of his.[10] Karzai was also in touch with Mullah Khairullah Khairkhwa, the governor of Herat (and released from Guantanamo Bay after 13 years in prison).[11] And Karzai knew Taliban prime minister Mullah Mohammad Rabbani (not to be confused with President Burhanuddin Rabbani), who had initiated the manhunt for the deposed communist president Najibullah that ended with his gruesome murder. Karzai called the action "unfortunate".[12] He believed Rabbani was a "modern Taliban leader."[13]

In 1994 Karzai had surprised the Western diplomats in Pakistan[14] He often dropped by their embassies to talk about his homeland, sometimes so frequently that the Westerners found it hard to devote so much time. For German diplomat Norbert Holl, the head of the UN mission in the region, Karzai was his 'main interlocutor'. Hamid came so often 'to talk about peace in Afghanistan' that Holl joked that the table they were sat around on would become historical if they managed to stop the war in Afghanistan. Yet the interviewed diplomats all say Karzai was only a mid-level player in terms of his influence, and that he wasn't the only Afghan to visit and ask for Western support. Norbert Holl says that Karzai, 'a man with limited potential', tried hard to bring new initiatives on a daily basis.

In 1994, however, Karzai's advice to the diplomats was that they should support the Taliban. American diplomat

Richard Smyth, the US consul general in Peshawar at that time, remembered him coming to his office. "Karzai said: 'they are disciplined, they have vision and its not based on parties like we have right now.' I think Karzai thought this system would help him also. To be any kind of leader, you are what the country needs at that time. Karzai was ambitious, for the good of the country, I think." Smyth was skeptical, but he asked Karzai to arrange a meeting with the Taliban. "That took a while, but he arranged it in the end." The Taliban asked for support according to Smyth, but the diplomat said they were not taking sides. Karzai went one step further with his friend Norbert Holl and asked him if he should work for the Taliban. "He went several times to Rome to meet the King in exile, but also met the Taliban in Gulf states." Holl said that "trying too many things at the same time would jeopardise his credibility". Karzai would ignore that advice and until the end of 1996 was in the race for a job with the Taliban.

*   *   *

HAMID KARZAI WAS born in 1957 as the last child of an affluent family. He had three older brothers (Abdul Ahmad, Qayoom, Mahmood) and one older sister Fauzia. His father Abdul Ahad was a respected Popolzai tribal elder until the early sixties, also working primarily in Kandahar and Uruzgan where their Popolzai tribe lives. For a short period he was governor of a district between Kandahar and Uruzgan, but in the sixties he left the south for Kabul, where he was appointed as a member of the senate. Hamid

Karzai's mother—from Kabul's Parwan—was also a Popolzai, coming from a rich family. Apparently, she broke the relationship with her husband Abdul Ahad Karzai in the sixties after he allegedly fell in love with a girl called Nazu from Argandab district in Kandahar, and married her against the will of Hamid Karzai's mother. Hamid Karzai's mother and his father were never formally divorced. The second marriage happened shortly after Hamid Karzai was born, and Abdul Ahad Karzai never really bonded with his son Hamid.[15]

The Western-oriented king Mohamed Zahir Shah had ruled in Kabul since the 1930s. He was a flamboyant man who would have liked to have been an artist instead. But when his father was murdered before his eyes in 1933, he had to take the throne. He was younger, but the government announced he had turned 18 and was old enough to become king.[16] By traditional Afghan standards, the new king proved to be quite modern. He had himself driven around in a Cadillac, frequently accompanied by Grace Kelly look-a-likes, and it's rumoured that his opposition to the female head scarf was so that he could see them better. The conservative Afghans considered him a heathen.

Zahir Shah wasn't a decisive man. Some Afghans appreciated this—with so many tribes, ethnic groups, and adjacent countries to contend with, one shouldn't be too ambitious. Diplomats, however, did get annoyed with his attitude. The reforms he initiated were slow to take place. Despite his lack of decisiveness, his reign was still considered a period of peace and tranquillity. It was the era when young Westerners with long hair and miniskirts coloured the streets of Kabul. But in those years an increasingly influential communist movement was developing, supported here and there by the Soviets, and Zahir Shah was dethrone 1 by his cousin in 1973 while away, visiting Rome. He chose to stay in Italy, a decision his followers resented. Under his cousin's rule, Afghanistan became a republic, and that was the end of the relative peace under the king.

The luxurious life enjoyed by many government officials was upended, and the Karzai clan wasn't spared. Even Karzai's father was reported to have done a stretch in prison. When the Red Army invaded in 1979, many leading families left the country, and Karzai's father went to Quetta. All his children went to the United States, except for Hamid, who never lived in the US, something many people (who see him as an 'American Puppet') find hard to believe. According to copies of his immigration papers that are seen by the author, in 1980 and again in 1982 Karzai did apply for a refugee status. He was invited twice to the American embassy in the Indian capital Delhi to talk about it. But there is no proof he got the paperwork finalised for his passports. Also, his family, and in particular Mahmoud Karzai, was wondering why he failed to attend the appointments with the American embassy. Mahmoud encouraged him to come live in the United States and advised him many times how to do that, but Hamid wasn't convinced.[17]

In 1977, Hamid Karzai went to India (not 1978 like his official biography states). He started to study Medicine in that year, but this didn't work out. He didn't attend his exams and in the summer of 1978 he went to Pakistan instead, never even finishing his first year to the disapproval of his brother Mahmoud.

His family was also against Karzai's choice to go back to India in 1978 and study Political Science instead. Hamid hardly discussed these issues with them and made the decision on his own. He didn't discuss the trip to India either with Mahmoud who sent him money for his stay.[18] Mahmoud told him that with medicine he could help Afghans or he could decide to come to the US where doctors earn a good salary.

Hamid Karzai didn't go to the US but started studying Political Science at the Himachal Pradesh University in India, where he also learned English. In the first year he was hardly present, and still travelled to Pakistan. His family noticed that his brother Hamid was more and more interested in the political situation in Afghanistan, where the Communists had taken over, and put Karzai's father in prison. Lots of young men joined the resistance against the Communists, and his family thought Hamid wanted that as well, and 'become more political'. His brothers asked him to spend less of the money he was sending for his studies because they couldn't afford to give him more. "I am in a poor situation", Mahmoud Karzai said who is now, through Karzai's presidency, a millionaire.

Mahmoud was also interested in studying medicine, but didn't have enough money. In those years he was still trying to make a living for himself together with the other brother, Qayoom, in the United States. In 1980, Karzai had a girlfriend, according to sources, but not much more is known. The author has seen a Bachelor-diploma of Political Science dedicated to Hamid Karzai, and also other entrance proof for the fourth semester of a master in Political Science he received with minimal marks. It's not clear if he finished his Masters.

A potential successor to his father, in 1983 he returned to Quetta indefinitely. At that time his brother Qayoom already visited Pakistan to join the Jihad. Qayoom wrote in late 1982 to Hamid in India that he didn't trust the United States and the Americans didn't want to leave Afghanistan because the war suited their interests. According to Qayoom, the Jihad was full of men who fight for their personal interest. It was time for an 'active political movement.'[19] But the Karzai clan's influence had been noticeably reduced. During the resistance against the Red Army, new rulers emerged who were well supplied with money and weapons, mainly by Pakistan and the United States. The Islamic conservative Gulbuddin Hekmatyar, supported mainly by Pakistanis, swiftly brought large parts of Afghanistan under his control. Mawlawi Mohammed Nabi Mohammedi, a member of the Afghan parliament under the king, also took up arms and gained the support of various Pashtuns. Another renowned resistance leader was the Islamist Younis Khalis, who had fled the king's regime. Khalis was purportedly involved in getting bin Laden into the country in 1996.

When Karzai returned from India, he started helping his father with the Jihad. To earn some money, he also got a job as an English teacher at IRC, an English language institute in Peshawar. According to some sources he also taught English in Quetta at the American Center. At the time, he was seen as an ordinary boy moving around the city on his bicycle, but because of his foreign language skills and his father's prominence, he soon became heavily engaged in the jihad against the Soviets. He interpreted at meetings with Afghans and Pakistanis at Western embassies, regularly arranging interviews, trips and other requests from journalists. It was only natural that he would become involved with the Afghan political parties from Pakistan. Karzai went back and forth between the two smallest parties, which were strongly oriented toward the West. Pakistan and the United States used them as conduits for funnelling weapons and money to the jihad. As a result, Karzai got increasing access to these foreign funds to support the fighting against the Red Army. He opened his own office in Quetta. While most of the attention went to the battle in the east, Karzai was focused more on the south and he distributed most of his dollars to the mujahedeen operating in the provinces of Kandahar and Uruzgan. He also journeyed to the battlefields in those areas himself, where he would call on fellow tribesmen like Jan Mohammed and others he would also enlist for his uprising in 2001. He occasionally had truckloads of food driven to his support base in Kandahar city and Tarin Kot. Through his good relations with the West he received letters from members of his own Jihad party and often also from Hizb-e Islami members who asked him for favours as well. He also managed to arrange medevac flights. A C-9A Nightingale aircraft would pick up the wounded, who were allowed to recuperate in America before returning to the fight.

Yet the Karzai clan didn't emerge as one of the strongest from the struggle against the Soviets. After the Red
Army left Afghanistan in 1989, a power struggle broke out
within the Popolzai tribe. The Karzais lost ground to Amir
Lalai from Kandahar, who received a key position in the
administration there. When Lalai demanded weapons and
money from the family, he reputedly slapped a Karzai
relative in the face.[20] For honour-sensitive Afghans it was a
grave humiliation. In their quest for control, the Karzai
clan relied increasingly on the remaining Popolzai, mainly
living in the next-door province, Uruzgan, where, thanks in
part to their support, fellow tribesman Jan Mohammed was
now in control. Jan Mohammed and the Karzai's have had
a very strong relationship since that time. Especially since
the commander Jan Mohammed had saved Karzai from an
assassination attempt in Tarin Kot in the late eighties,
Hamid Karzai was indebted to him for life. The co-
dependency that had developed between the two men was
only strengthened by Amir Lalai's slap. Until 2000, when
Jan Mohammed would end up in the Taliban-prison,
Hamid Karzai coordinated most of his work with this
poorly educated man from Uruzgan.

Despite the outcome of the Kandahar power struggle,
Hamid Karzai obtained a position in the cabinet in Kabul.
This happened under the leadership of what became
known as the Northern Alliance, which had established
itself in Kabul after the Soviets left. Hamid Karzai's father
apparently had refused the job – he didn't respect the new
leaders – and had his youngest son appointed since Hamid
Karzai had fewer problems with it.[21] He was appointed

deputy minister of foreign affairs—not a key position, but it did give him a diplomatic passport. The position didn't last long because he soon fell out with President Burhanuddin Rabbani, who saw his own authority dwindle as Afghanistan descended into civil war.[22]

When the Taliban first appeared on the stage in 1994, Karzai was enthusiastic about the new movement. For the Karzai-family, the movement also meant new opportunities in the battle against Amir Lalai, who had strongly resisted the Taliban. After he lost a bloody battle near Kandahar and found his man hanging on the barrel of a tank, he fled to Iran. Some of Lalai's warriors then switched their allegiances to the Karzai clan who hoped to become powerful again with the help of the Taliban. So Karzai handed over his weapons, munitions and US$50,000 to the new leaders.[23]

Thanks in part to his support of the Taliban, Karzai became a candidate for the position of United Nations ambassador for the Taliban administration.[24] It was a tit-for-tat deal. His father, Abdul Ahad Karzai, had supported these tribally-related Taliban in early meetings in 1994 in Quetta and in Kandahar, and wanted something in return. The Taliban of the Popolzai-related tribes offered the UN post to the youngest son. But however generous Karzai was toward the Taliban, he couldn't gain the trust of the senior Taliban rulers or Mullah Omar himself. He first sent his half-brother Ahmed Wali Karzai to Yar Mohammed (Popolzai Taliban) and then to Mullah Ghaus (Popolzai Taliban) who were both in Kandahar. Please let him be the UN ambassador, his half-brother said. Both said that

Mullah Omar didn't support the idea. After another visit, Mullah Ghaus said: Mullah Omar prefers a little Taliban over Hamid Karzai, sorry.[25] In the meantime the lobbying for Karzai went on in Kabul and an approval letter was drawn up in the ministry of foreign affairs. But the author of the letter told me it was never sent to the UN headquarters in New York. "Mullah Omar had problems with trusting Hamid Karzai. He had too many links with the foreigners." Also staff members in the ministry had doubts. "He is working for the CIA, I am sure", they assumed.[26]

By the end of 1996, after it became clear Hamid Karzai would not get a job at the UN, Karzai was in the office of the US Secretary of State in Washington, begging for American support for 'modern, educated Afghans'. "It's the only way to weaken the Taliban's views," he argued. It was obvious that the Popolzai Taliban were losing influence, and Hamid Karzai wanted to intervene. To Karzai, the other Taliban were "a group of simple, undereducated people" who would throw Afghanistan into international isolation with their conservative policies. Although an American ambassador promised Karzai he would discuss the matter with the Taliban, he also said the Americans would not support any one group in the Afghan conflict.[27]

Meanwhile Karzai's father had grown increasingly annoyed with his son's behaviour.[28] Family friends say that it really bothered the elder Karzai that his son made no clear-cut choices. He wanted to be friends with everyone: with America, with Pakistan, with the Taliban, with the old warlords, and with the royal family who were still in Rome. The American ambassador Richard Smyth said that it was

Hamid who reached out to them, not Abdul Ahad. "I wasn't talking to his father, because it was too hard to get him." Hamid also intensified his grip as patriarch of the Karzai clan, and in Quetta he met with several influential people without including his father. It's said that tension often rose so high in the Karzai residence that father Abdul Ahad regularly called his son a donkey and sometimes told others that he feared his son wasn't all there.[29]

The Karzai's non-profit organisation, Environmental Awareness Federation of Afghanistan (EAFA), was created by Qayoom Karzai in the early nineties and continued operating during the Taliban time with a spacious office in Kandahar city. Again, the Popolzai Taliban Yar Mohammed and Abdul Jalil supported them. "You can stay, don't worry", he told one of the interviewed employees of EAFA. For several projects EAFA got accreditation letters from the Taliban. From the administration of EAFA seen by the author, it's clear Ahmad Wali was often in Kandahar to take care of dozens of development projects in mostly only Popolzai areas in Uruzgan and Kandahar. It's unclear why the Karzai's mostly helped their network of tribal people, except that it gave them credibility as family. Also, the Popolzai Talib Mullah Ghaus got a project – a dam – in his area in Char Chino in the Taliban time. The World Health Organisation and several UN-organisations were funding these EAFA programs. It was mainly Hamid Karzai who arranged the funds after his visits to the Western organisations based in Islamabad. According to an employee he just 'snapped his fingers' and the international community agreed to work with them.

While helping his own people with development projects and jobs, Karzai also became more politically active. After he was rejected as an UN ambassador, he became part of the opposition against the senior leadership of the Taliban, people like Mullah Omar. After al-Qaeda's attacks on the American embassies in Nairobi and Dar-es-Salaam in 1998, his relations with the Americans, who were seeking new allies in the fight against Osama bin Laden, grew closer. He also invited old Uruzgani tribesmen to Quetta more frequently to discuss Afghanistan's future. He arranged visas for old mujahedeen who were driven out by the Taliban, so that they could attend conferences on Afghanistan in places like Frankfurt, Istanbul or the United States.[30] Two hundred Afghans attended a conference in Germany in 1998. Interestingly, Taliban delegates had been invited to the conference as well. So it would seem that Karzai and his allies made a distinction between the native Taliban and al-Qaeda, which were perceived by many Afghans to be a foreign invading power. But the Taliban weren't interested. Although representatives of the exiled king in Rome frequently went to Kandahar to talk with them, the discussions went nowhere. In 1999, around two months after Hamid Karzai's mother died of cancer, Karzai's father was murdered. He had recently returned from America when on July 14 two gunmen shot him to death from a passing motorcycle as he walked to the mosque. Though the media and the family itself blamed the Taliban, the motives for his murder were never clear. Was it the Taliban? A family rival? The Americans sent their condolences. He was buried in Kandahar. Karzai, who had received death threats from one group of Taliban, was able to attend the funeral under the protection of his own connections with the Taliban. He arrived secretly in the night and brought his father's dead body to the cemetery the next morning. He didn't have a lot of time; the Taliban's militia were on their way to surround Karzai's EAFA office in Kandahar, ready to attack. Karzai was warned, and fled from his father's funeral to return to Quetta.[31] Ahmad Wali, his half-brother, had better connections in Kandahar and stayed on.

The issue of succession brought on a bloody feud inside Karzai's family. It all started with the earlier murder of the step-brother of Karzai's father by another family member, Yar Mohammed. The killing tore the family apart, and its effects are still felt to this day. Karzai's step-father had refused to marry a daughter to Yar Mohammed's family. Since then, the family of the murdered stepbrother and Karzai's other nieces were on the path of revenge. So when they started to look for a successor to take up the helm after Abdul Ahad, all this came out. In the meeting in Quetta where tribal leaders came together to decide, Hashmat Karzai – son of the murdered step-brother—said that he deserved the leadership of the family. Jan Mohammed intervened on behalf of Hamid Karzai and won. "What a motherfucker," Ahmed Wali Karzai whispered to his assistant when Hashmat left. When the Taliban came to power in 1994, Hashmat convinced the Taliban that Yar Mohammed – the murderer of his father – was in opposition to them and Yar Mohammed was thrown in Taliban-prison. Yar Mohammed only laughed about it, the rumour goes. "Why not kill me he?" he said, accusing Hashmat of being weak. Soon Karzai was appointed as his father's successor. The tribal leaders draped a *patu* around him. Then a knot was tied in the shawl to confirm his status as his father's successor.

Karzai continued to drop in at the U.S. Embassy in Islamabad on a regular basis, often accompanied by Jan Mohammed and 'his' men from Uruzgan and Kandahar.[32] They told the Americans they planned to organise military resistance against the Taliban from Uruzgan, as had previously been done successfully against the Red Army. The Russians supported the Northern Alliance in the fight against the Taliban, and Iran supported ethnic groups like the Hazara. So the Americans could do something similar in the south, they argued. To Jan Mohammed, the mountainous terrain was ideal for quietly building up *lashkars*, or tribal militias. Before their plans could be set in motion he was betrayed, arrested by the Taliban, and imprisoned – and with that Karzai's principal support in southern Afghanistan evaporated.

Karzai persevered. In 2000 he sought contact with the Northern Alliance.[33] It was an unusual step, especially given his history with the group. Many Pashtuns believed that the Tajiks, Uzbeks, and Hazara who were the Northern Alliance had no right to any power since Afghanistan, after all, was established by Pashtuns. But it was typical of Karzai to keep his options open, eventually sealing an agreement with the Alliance's leader, Ahmad Shah Massoud, about mutual support. The initiative could count on political support from the State Department in Washington, although Massoud was controversial. He was indeed a famous military leader, but his people were also accused of being involved in drugs smuggling. Also their human rights record was questionable. Karzai started working with more dubious strongmen too, people he needed desperately, and who would get rewarded after 2001, when Karzai brought all of them into his government. Among them was the Uzbek, Abdul Rashid Dostum—a notorious warrior in the civil war around Kabul who fled the Taliban. Another was Ismael Khan, who had been governor in Herat province before the Taliban took over, subsequently escaping from the Taliban prison in Kandahar city and fleeing to Iran, before finally returning to Afghanistan. The Hazara leader Karim Khalili, who maintained a low profile in central Afghanistan's Bamyan province, was yet another controversial leader. Finally there was Haji Qadir, a strongmen and politician from Jalalabad who had already created a small militia of his own.

With the foreign diplomats, Hamid Karzai was the educated, English-speaking and well-mannered raconteur, who received New Year's wishes by card from the American ambassadors. In Afghanistan, Hamid Karzai was different, making alliances with war criminals and strongmen. He knew he needed them and for that he studied maps with Massoud to determine how they could set up the military resistance.[34] Massoud sent all his information about al-Qaeda to the CIA but ousting the Taliban was his main priority. He intended to build up pockets of resistance here and there in the north and west. As soon as the Taliban reacted to these little flash points, he would move against them with more heavily armed militias. It was also part of the plan to include Uruzgan in these pockets of resistance. Massoud already understood that moving directly on Kandahar city wasn't an option. They also discussed how best to free Jan Mohammed from prison. It was important that he joined Massoud's cadre of insurgents. They agreed that the men Karzai gathered in Uruzgan would go to the north using the Panjshir Valley—a beautiful, verdant region that wasn't yet in Taliban hands—as their starting point. After that, these men and Massoud would establish operations in the south, perhaps in the mountains of Uruzgan, and slowly move toward Kandahar.

The Americans were only mildly concerned with driving out the Taliban.[35] They were more focused on bin Laden, who had been operating under Taliban protection in Afghanistan since 1996. He was considered the brains behind the attacks in Nairobi, Dar-es-Salaam and the more recent attack on the *USS Cole*, a US Navy destroyer. "We want Osama bin Laden," the Americans told Karzai repeatedly. "And you must negotiate with the Taliban about his extradition." Karzai told them he had little faith that negotiations with the Taliban would work. Bin Laden's home country Saudi Arabia had asked the Taliban to hand him over and had even offered US$400 million. Although this led to some discussion within the Taliban, they ended up turning down the offer, claiming it was their Islamic duty to offer hospitality to their Muslim brother.

Although the issue was controversial at the State Department, the Americans continued to push for a dialogue with the Taliban. There were no plans for regime change.[36]

Yet Karzai remained in touch with the United States because he was convinced that only America had the ability to change anything in Afghanistan. But it was challenging. Afghanistan simply wasn't on the radar. The Americans did what Pakistan wanted. "You are very nice intellectuals, but you had better go and deal with the Taliban," the Americans kept telling Karzai. When Pakistan wanted to stop Karzai and sent Karzai a letter saying he wouldn't get his visa extended after September 2001, Karzai was able to rely on the help of the US. "At that point," he said, "I think the US intervened and told Pakistan not to expel me. But I don't know if it had an effect. I told the US that I was expelled, and [asked] if they could help. I am sure they did something."[37]

FOUR

This Is Suicide: Serious Doubts in Karzai's Group

D URING THE LAST week of September 2001 Karzai was seated across from an ageing man with dark eyes and a weathered face.[38] He was one of the men that Said had called, at Karzai's request, from Uruzgan to Quetta. Originally from the small river hamlet Lundyana near Deh Rawud, he had been named after the patriarch Abraham, and his name–Ibrahim–fit his nature. A Popolzai, he knew Karzai and even belonged to the same sub-tribe. In recent years he had been to Quetta, sometimes at Karzai's emphatic request. "Do you still support me?" Karzai would ask, and on each occasion Ibrahim had nodded yes. He was now back in Quetta to listen to his elder. Karzai declared that, "the world no longer wants the Taliban" and that it was time to join hands for change. As usual, Ibrahim listened to him patiently, although he didn't really understand. He barely comprehended what had happened halfway across the globe on 9/11. Eventually he offered a few words. "But the Taliban is strong, you know—how can we do anything now?" Karzai blew off his objections. "Don't worry," he told Ibrahim. "I have spoken with the world."

Karzai gave him a list of names. Ibrahim's eyes were weak and he had to hold the paper at arm's length to read what was written on it. The names were of Afghans from his own region of Deh Rawud: clansmen, Taliban, ex-Taliban, everyone. He knew them all. Karzai didn't need to explain to Ibrahim what he wanted from him. Like Said, he had to take the message from Quetta to the *kalas* of his acquaintances and kin and meet with these men. But he received more information than Said had a few days ago—much more. He had to prepare these men's minds for change in his province. Karzai wanted to get "inside" to initiate changes himself and Ibrahim's role was to clear the way for him. Ibrahim, who had fought for years at the front lines against the Soviets, wearily ran his hands though his hair. "This is playing with fire," he said. He didn't mind a revolt; that wasn't what bothered him. He didn't think it was a good idea for Karzai to return to Uruzgan himself. There was too much at stake. In Ibrahim's eyes Karzai was his tribal elder, and his death would be disastrous. He was convinced it would be suicide. But Karzai wasn't listening and eventually Ibrahim agreed to carry out Karzai's wishes.

Ibrahim was not the only one with doubts about Karzai's plans. "We have no weapons," someone else had already pointed out to Karzai. "How do you think you can get into Uruzgan?" yet another man asked. Still, Karzai didn't change his mind. These men had the right kind of connections and he was banking on them. They were the nodes within the social tribal networks and he intended to use them for his mission. He was convinced that fighting was a hopeless strategy, since the Taliban were much too strong in the Pashtun region.[39] Therefore they would have to influence the people in Uruzgan and other southern provinces. Not by killing them, but by talking. That was the beginning. Only if it didn't work violence could be used, with support from the Americans. This was also why Karzai wished to take the lead in the revolt himself—he wanted to be the alternative to the Taliban.

"I will be the flag bearer," Karzai said. "How can you do that without fighting?" one of the men from Uruzgan immediately asked him. But Karzai ignored the question. "You are like brothers to me, but if you murder a Taliban follower, I will chop your heads off," the men heard him say.[40]

Many Afghan leaders have employed Karzai's 'soft approach' to the expansion of power. Previous Afghan leaders like Amir Abdur Rahman, used the same tactics in the eighteenth century. He first arranged the support of a small group of close family and tribesmen. With them on board, Abdur Rahman marched on Kandahar by sending hundreds of letters to other tribes to get their support, promising them full protection, weapons, exemption from tax and other privileges. He alone arranged money from the British in India to fulfil these promises.[41]

The same approach had been tried in recent Afghan history. When the jihad against the Soviets began. Small groups of tribal leaders, or *jirgas*, would travel from *kota* to *kota* with supplies, gifts, and money to gather support. Loyalties aren't fixed.[42] On the contrary, it's considered a benefit when a family network expands to include both sides of a political divide. One day something can be arranged with the administration, the next day with the other side. This is characteristic for the Pashtun: risk is distributed, and it's the result, not political convictions, that counts.

To outsiders it's therefore not immediately obvious where a Pashtun's loyalties lie in a potpourri of sub-tribes, with networks that are extremely complex. The Pashtun have a tradition of *tarbourwali*, for example, which treats rivalry as a virtue, even within families. Competition between cousins and sometimes even brothers determines how power is distributed within the clan. From an early age boys are taught to defend their honour in the *kotas*. Physical violence between these boys is not unusual. This constant contention means one can always find an extended family member – an underdog –willing to form new alliances. The trade in weapons during the jihad against the Soviets intensified such rivalries. In these battles for dominance, religion or political convictions hardly mattered. To many Afghans, regime change represents new opportunities for advancement within clan or tribe.

One of Karzai's insurgent allies in Uruzgan, the Barakzai leader Rozi Khan, observed that their tribal politics had less and less effect under the Taliban. The regime was reasonably successful at minimising such battles and handling other problems, such as theft or even murder, informally and among themselves.[43] "When we were still in control," says Rozi Khan, "and someone was murdered, you talked to the victim's elder or warlord and he would solve the problem. During the Taliban it was the other way around. The Taliban ignored the elders and brought in administrators from outside. We often had no connections to them. So if you stole something, there was no one supporting you. The same with murder. The Taliban would bring the murderer before a judge, who would have him summarily executed. Because regular Afghans couldn't give their side of the story, they were more afraid of the Taliban than of their previous tribal elders. When there was a disagreement concerning land or water, they would simply let it go."

Rozi Khan still had some connections within the Taliban, but those were increasingly difficult to exploit. He managed to keep his own weapons out of Taliban hands and hide them in northern Uruzgan. One of his friends in the Taliban, Haji Houdoud, protected him but that wasn't always enough. Houdoud wrote a friendly letter stating Rozi Khan had no more weapons, but the weapons checks continued. At regular intervals new Taliban groups would show up with the urgent request that he hand in his gear. On a few occasions it got too dangerous for him, and he would go to Kabul for a while.

The former Uruzgan police chief Aziz started having problems with the Taliban too. Not only because Aziz opposed the Taliban ideologically, but it was also a matter of power. The Taliban kept an eye on Aziz who represented the regime they toppled. But Aziz's *tarbour*, a rival cousin, also created problems. This cousin was restricted when Aziz was police commander, but had taken advantage of the rise of the new regime. Previously the 'underdog' in the family, the cousin could finally take revenge. Even with small things he wouldn't leave Aziz's family alone. When Aziz built an irrigation canal for his orchard, his cousin, who lived around the corner, demanded that he extend it. When he refused, the relationship between the two became difficult. In fit of rage, the cousin blocked the way to Aziz's *kala* with a large rock. While Aziz attended a major opposition conference in Germany, his cousin made additional trouble back home, to the point that Aziz decided to take refuge. During Aziz's absence, the tarbour dropped by the *kota* every day to ask where the master of the house was. To the family's dismay, these unexpected visits increased when he got no answer. The Taliban (read: his rival cousin) entered without knocking, sometimes at three in the morning. The *kota* would be full of sleeping guests, but the cousin didn't care. In order to get Aziz back to Afghanistan, in part at Hamid Karzai's request, the family sought an appeal with a Taliban tribal member. The acquaintance, an influential man from Kandahar, still owed Aziz for a trip to Mecca he once sponsored. Fifteen representatives of the Aziz family went to the Taliban for advice. They told him that Aziz had been in a Western hospital. Only after the men had personally convinced the Taliban leader Mullah Omar of this story was Aziz able to return to Tarin Kot.

Under the Taliban, traditional forms of nepotism were rendered ineffectual, and former governor Jan Mohammed was hit hardest by the change. After the Taliban had taken over in Uruzgan, he tried to stay in touch with the U.S. Embassy in Islamabad but it was increasingly difficult to keep these visits hidden from the new rulers. At first he would bribe a Mullah to announce on the radio that Jan Mohammed wasn't a threat to the Taliban. In Quetta he had staged pictures taken of old wounds to prove he had been to Pakistan for medical treatment. But despite all his attempts to cheat, the once powerful strongman lost. One of his friends eventually betrayed him and he ended up as a prisoner of the Taliban, until they were driven out in 2001.

Apart from the fact that the previous warlords and elders' control had dwindled, it was still unclear how great the dissatisfaction with the Taliban regime was among other people in Uruzgan.[44] The province finally had peace and order after years of corrupt leaders and tribal feuds. Granted, fundamentalist rules regarding compulsory mosque attendance and the prescribed fist-long beard was a bother. Some men were detained because their beards were the wrong length. Listening to music was also harshly punished. Yet in some ways the Taliban policies were consistent with the views of the province's population. Take the *burqa*. Women in Afghanistan often wore the garment even before the Taliban rose to power. Judicial sentences of stoning took place, especially in large cities such as Kabul and Kandahar (where the Taliban were generally more radical) but not in Uruzgan. Schools for girls were closed under Taliban rule, but outside of centres like Tarin Kot and Deh Rawud the Taliban pretty much left the countryside alone.[45] There, women were allowed to wear just their headscarves instead of *burqas*. And in the few Shi'ite Hazara villages, girls continued to go to school.

One thing that led to tremendous dissatisfaction was the draft. Families had to send their first-born sons to the battle against the Northern Alliance. Many boys tried to evade the draft, but not all succeeded. Countless young boys would be lined up at the small hospital in Tarin Kot. From there the same helicopters that brought back the dead and wounded ferried them to Uruzgan. This led to dramatic scenes of crying mothers watching their healthy sons leave for the front while others watched their dead sons return.

*　　*　　*

LIKE IBRAHIM, ABDUL Ghani also accepted the invitation he received through the messenger Said. He was from Kot Wal village, north of Tarin Kot. A short man with black curls and a long beard, he was a local leader who had earned the nickname "Mama", which means something like "maternal uncle." He was irritated and puzzled at Karzai's invitation. He had travelled back and forth to Quetta in recent years to meet with the elder Karzai, and later with his son Hamid. This time he wasn't allowed to join the regular guests in the *kota*. Suspicious, he wondered at the meaning of it. But Abdul Ghani hadn't always been Karzai's friend. Until the Taliban took over he was allied with Amir Lalai, the Karzai family's principal adversary. Unlike the Karzais, Lalai had initially resisted the Taliban, before fleeing to Iran. Only then had Abdul Ghani switched to Karzai's side. When Karzai joined him after several hours, he tested his loyalty. Karzai told him the Taliban were finished. Abdul Ghani could hardly believe it. "What do you mean?" he asked. "That's impossible." The

Taliban had treated him harshly these past years; all his weapons had been confiscated and he would sit at home, powerless. But Karzai insisted. He spoke of the distant, mighty America he believed was going to intervene in Afghanistan. "Much will change," said Karzai. "We must serve our country now and everyone must participate." Abdul Ghani still didn't know what to think of Karzai's message. What does that mean, America supports us? What does Karzai really want? Does he appreciate how difficult it is to begin anything against the Taliban in Uruzgan?

Ibrahim and Abdul Ghani's skepticism was shared by all the men who had come to Quetta. They hardly understood what had just happened to the Twin Towers, or, by extension, to Afghanistan's place in the world. To them America was still the country that supported them in the fight against the Soviets before disappearing from the scene. In recent years, attempts to get weapons and money from the Americans for the struggle against the Taliban had failed time and again.

Haji Bahadur had similar doubts when he arrived at Karzai's *kala* in Quetta. Like Jan Mohammed, Haji Bahadur was a member of the Karanag subtribe, which meant he was more closely related to Karzai than were most of the others. Although he was one of the youngest invitees, he had made a name for himself in the fight against the Soviets. Bahadur was not his given name, but an honorific meaning "Hero" that he had earned on the battlefield. Together with his brother – Haji Zahir Agha – he also fought a vicious tribal battle in his own region after the war, which resulted in the massacre of at least three rival families (in earlier times these rival families killed people of Bahadur's), and which allowed the clan to appropriate a lot of land. Despite his cruelty, Karzai trusted this closely related tribesman and asked him several times to accompany him to the U.S. Embassy in Islamabad. Like the others, Bahadur also heard from Karzai that the Americans would now change their previously passive approach toward the Taliban. "In America events have taken place which have made them extremely angry with the Taliban," he explained to Bahadur. "If we go in at this point to drive out the Taliban, the Americans will support us with their fighter jets," Karzai said. Despite his doubts, Haji Bahadur was gradually persuaded that Karzai was not talking nonsense.

The 'weapons' Karzai planned to use in Uruzgan were unusual, though. "What's this?" asked Haji Bahadur when a black contraption was shoved into his hands. "This is a telephone," says Karzai. "It has buttons which I will explain to you all." Bahadur had never used such a thing. It must have been an amusing sight, the Uruzganis with state of the art satellite telephones in tiny black suitcases with antennae on the lid. "You have to aim this antenna toward the sun," Karzai explained, alluding to the satellites for telephone communication. Some would never learn to use them; still, Karzai insisted that the telephones are crucial. Once back in Uruzgan, he intended to stay in constant contact with his men. He wanted regular updates concerning the talks taking place in the Uruzgani *kotas*. How many Taliban had surrendered so far? Had this leader or that cousin been in touch yet? In order to understand the situation it was imperative that he hand out as many of those little black boxes as possible.

Like many others, Haji Bahadur returns to Uruzgan with satellite telephones and with some already familiar walkie-talkies. The men had to distribute these means of communication within their own networks. In some cases the men didn't take the telephones themselves, but had them delivered later by anonymous messengers, thereby avoiding the inevitable checkpoints. In addition Karzai gave each man about 10,000 to 20,000 Pakistani rupees (about US$170 to US$350), meant for travel expenses and to buy their loyalty.

FIVE

America Takes Revenge

A FEW DAYS after September 11, 2001, US President George W. Bush addressed the nation. "We will find those who did it; we will smoke them out of their holes. We will get them running and we'll bring them to justice. There is a desire by the American people to not seek only revenge, but to win a war against barbaric behaviour."[46] By now the Americans were certain the attacks, which killed approximately three thousand, were the work of Osama bin Laden and al-Qaeda, operating out of Afghanistan. They had America's full attention.

The search for Bin Laden began in the north.[47] There was still a small sliver of land there that wasn't under Taliban control, and it was the only place where the Americans could enter Afghanistan. Although the Northern Alliance had repeatedly asked the Americans for military assistance, the Americans had not shown much interest. After 9/11 everything changed, but simply getting into the country was a challenge.

Two days before 9/11, the Northern Alliance leader, Ahmad Shah Massoud, was murdered. Two Arabs from Brussels, Belgium, posing as journalists, managed to get close to him and detonated a bomb hidden in their camera. Al-Qaeda was alleged to have been behind the assassination. The group would have assumed that after the attacks on the Twin Towers the US would start a war in Afghanistan and would need help from the Northern Alliance. By killing Massoud, bin Laden would pre-emptively undermine the morale of the Alliance forces.

On September 17, US President Bush signed a bill making US$1 billion available for this secret war. Most of the action would take place away from the cameras, Bush warned. It was already difficult for journalists to get visas to enter Afghanistan. At the same time Karzai sent Said to Uruzgan, the first CIA team arrived secretly by helicopter at the Northern Alliance headquarters. With millions of dollars to hand out, the CIA hoped to mobilise the group in the hunt for bin Laden and the Taliban. The American secret agents had an unambiguous mission: "I want to see pictures of Osama bin Laden's head on a stake," their boss had told them. "And then I want his head brought here on ice so I can show it to the president."

The U.S. Embassy in Pakistan also had plenty of money to distribute to Afghans willing to help the Americans in their mission. But all didn't exactly share the enthusiasm. Several elders and warlords had fought hard in the war against the Soviets, and they were supported by America, but once the mutual enemy had been driven out, they never heard from America again. Many potential insurgents were drawn to the dollars, but they took a wait-and-see approach. The satellite phones the Americans distributed ended up on the black market in Pakistan. It was discovered that at least one opposition leaders bought a very expensive car and built a nice house for US$1 million.[48]

There were exceptions, such as Abdul Haq, a former mujahedeen leader operating in eastern Afghanistan who was strongly opposed to the Taliban.[49] He lost a leg in the war against the Soviets. Under the Taliban regime he came home one day to find his wife and child killed. He claimed he already had thousands of armed men available—at least a third of them were the first defectors from the Taliban. Haq wanted to prevent the Northern Alliance from taking all the power in Afghanistan with American assistance. He intended to enter the country without foreign support and oust the Taliban.

At this point, Hamid Karzai was largely out of the picture. Journalists knew him mainly as a helpful diplomat who did odd jobs and interpreted during the Soviet era. He didn't seem the kind of man to lead an armed opposition movement.

While the money started to flow in the north and in Islamabad, Karzai, like many other leaders in Quetta, was meeting secretly with the CIA. He approached a secret agent who called himself Graig.[50] He and Karzai already knew one another from before 9/11, and had met a few times in Quetta.[51] But now the atmosphere was much more upbeat. Many times the US and also Graig had disappointed Karzai, but now they were willing to help. In the Serena Hotel in Quetta, where the red-haired American received 'numerous' Afghans, they discussed options for entering Uruzgan.[52] (Graig would later become the CIA station chief in Kabul) He provided Hamid Karzai support in the form of money and satellite phones, although it was uncertain whether the CIA agreed with Karzai's plans. A colleague of Graig's, then part of the CIA team in the north, asserted that the CIA actually advised him to wait for help from an American commando team. Karzai ignored the advice.[53] "I had asked them for help before 9/11 and I asked for it again after. I didn't tell the CIA the exact date I went in. That was too dangerous and could leak to the ISI."

The comings and goings of Afghan visitors in Karzai's *kala* in Quetta were only mentioned by a few Pakistani media outlets; international journalists barely noticed Karzai at all. One article by the American journalist Molly Moore in the *Washington Post*— based on Pakistani accounts—mentions him as the potential new Afghan president. "Pakistani newspapers have speculated that Karzai is campaigning for a presidential nomination with his coalition-building talks."[54] Karzai dismissed the suggestion in the same article. Moore's colleague, the Pakistani journalist Ahmed Rashid, didn't share her theory.[55] Rashid had spoken to the Americans, to the British, and to United Nations people in Islamabad, he said. "They didn't take him seriously," said Rashid, who believed instead that the articles in the Pakistani media were a trap, planted to direct Taliban attention to Karzai's intentions toward them.

Guido Rampoldi, an Italian reporter with *La Repubblica* who visited Karzai in Quetta, asked him directly what his ambitions were. "Karzai was excited after the attacks. He immediately understood that history would take a turn and he was pleased for Afghanistan. When I asked him:

'Are you the new leader?' he didn´t answer. He only said that now everyone must participate again. He would even sit down with Gulbuddin Hekmatyar if need be."[56]

According to Rampoldi, the Americans didn't consider him the potential president at that time. "In my opinion they felt he had to prove himself first. Still it didn't seem impossible to me that he would emerge as the leader. Afghan history shows that Kandahar generates a lot of leaders and that they are usually Pashtuns. Karzai had worked hard for his country's future. He was a genuine patriot and he had good connections with the Americans. That was essential now."

At the beginning of October, Karzai sent another messenger to the elders in Uruzgan. Mohammed Shah was viewed by many in Afghanistan as an extension of Karzai himself. Officially he was Karzai's security guard, but in recent years he had been given the authority to welcome people in the *kota* on Karzai's behalf. In those instances he often functioned as a kind of personal secretary, operating relatively independently when it came to uncomplicated matters. Karzai also frequently discussed options for entering the south with him. So for Shah, Karzai's plans weren't new.[57]

Karzai and Shah were a remarkable duo. Shah had nothing in common with the calm, highly educated Karzai. His appearance was that of a typical proud Kandahari—he has a loud, harsh voice, a pitted face, bright green eyes, tattoos, and he was missing a piece of one of his thumbs. He had a reputation for being fearless and somewhat unreliable. He was from the same tribe as Karzai, and he claimed that he had married into Karzai's clan. There were years when their relationship wasn't as close. When the Taliban appeared, Shah was aligned with Karzai's rival Lalai. After Lalai fled from the Taliban to Iran, Shah turned to Karzai. So it took a while for Karzai to trust him, and for a period it was even forbidden for Shah to enter Karzai's *kota*. Still, Shah guarded Karzai's *kala* against intruders and regularly accompanied Karzai when he went jogging near the military base outside Quetta, driving their car to the main entrance and waiting until Karzai returned from his workout. Afterward they would often drink a cup of tea at the luxurious Serena Hotel in the city.

Shah understood Karzai's plans better than most. He grasped what had happened on September 11. He watched the televisions in Karzai's *kala* for hours on end, and understood that the Americans would soon intervene in Afghanistan. But like the men from Uruzgan, Shah also believed Karzai would do well to stay in Quetta. He saw grave perils for the man famous for never having held a gun. "I will go in, no problem," he said, but he felt that it was far too dangerous for his boss. But Karzai would not be dissuaded.

Shah, too, received a little black suitcase with a satellite phone from Karzai. "I will explain to you how it works," said Karzai. The same evening he called Shah at his home a few blocks away; later, Shah would return the call. The following day Shah also received a big bag full of Pakistani rupees – enough to bribe a few fighters. That same day Karzai accompanied Shah to the bus stop where they flagged down a taxi that would take him to mountainous

Uruzgan via Kandahar. He knew where he was going: to his friend Abdul Ghani, who had returned to Uruzgan from Quetta a few days earlier. For security reasons the satellite phone remained behind and would be delivered later by Said.

SIX

Crossing Taliban Territory on a Motorcycle

A FEW MEN sat listlessly against the wall in Abdul Ghani's *kala*, children playing at their feet while others ran around energetically. Every now and then they refilled the men's dirty glasses with hot tea. On any given day men would sit here to discuss the news, to resolve family conflicts, or simply to engage in idle conversation. This wasn't such an occasion. It was late at night and their host, Abdul Ghani, had locked the door of the high *kala* wall. No one else would be let in. In a break with normal courtesies, the door to the *kota* was also locked. People might speculate as to what was going on behind the high walls of the locked *kala*, and gossip would have been devastating.

Mohammed Shah was present at Abdul Ghani's dimly lit room. He had just arrived from Quetta and had expected support from his old friend. It was immediately evident that there were problems. Abdul Ghani was alarmed to see Shah at his door and he even tried to send him away. His older brother intervened. "Let him in," he said sternly. Ghani meekly obeyed and had tea poured for Shah. Now that Karzai's right hand man has made his appearance in the village, it was clear that Karzai was serious. Ghani still had doubts about his plans, but he sensed he could no longer avoid the issue. Shah had barely recovered from the long trip from Quetta when he began to discuss those plans. Ghani would have preferred not to hear any of it, but the Kandahari's hoarse voice repeated the same message: Karzai intends to revolt and you have to support him.

Shah explained the strategy to the men in the *kala*. "You aren't supposed to spend this on yourselves," he said, holding up a bag full of Pakistani rupees with one hand. "This money is meant for recruiting young men," he said before putting the money back down. "You men must send your messengers into the desert, to other villages, to other loyal kin, to announce Karzai's arrival."

Shah noticed that Karzai's earlier appeals to spread his message in other villages throughout the province had been ignored. The satellite phone was turned off, its little black suitcase lying unused in the room's alcove. Here in Kot Wal the men didn't have much faith in a former diplomat who wanted to start an uprising. Even though many in Quetta now understood the implications of 9/11, the same was not true of this audience. They had a hard time believing the Americans had plans for Afghanistan. And so Shah had his work cut out for him. He divided the rupees among the men, and bills passed from hand to hand. To give them an extra push Shah had the Koran brought out. It was quite common for agreements to be sealed by swearing on the holy book. The Koran was placed in the middle of the *kota* and Shah asked the men to place their hands on it. No one refused. The teacups were moved to the side and everyone sat up straight. They placed their hands on the Koran. They swore they would join the uprising and support Karzai's plans for a new future.

A few days after the men placed their hands on the Koran in Abdul Ghani's *kala*, proof of American intentions came falling from the dark sky. On October 7, 2001, at 21:10 local time, Operation Enduring Freedom began. There had been some uncertainty about when the attack would take place. The CIA team in the north expected Washington to take action earlier.[58] One Taliban leader or al-Qaeda operative after the next was fleeing to Pakistan. There had been some delay at first as Pakistan tried to persuade its old ally Mullah Omar to hand bin Laden over peacefully. In the mean time Mullah Omar secretly had tried to arrange with the CIA Bin Laden's transfer to a neutral third country, but Washington demanded an uncondtioonal handover. For two days, leading Pakistanis and Taliban leaders conferred about the extradition. While the Americans had high hopes, messengers from Pakistani president Musharraf did the opposite. They warned Mullah Omar of the plans of the US to invade, so he could prepare himself. Within the ISI (the Pakistani secret service) chaos reigned. Some helped the Americans by pointing out possible targets while others swiftly transferred truckloads of weapons, munitions and fuel to Kandahar to reinforce the Taliban.

Finally, on the night of October 7, thirty-one targets were attacked from the air. The American military tried to destroy strategic Taliban and al-Qaeda positions with air strikes, particularly in Kabul and Kandahar, bombers dispatched from a base in the American state of Missouri and a British island in the Indian Ocean. Submarines launched cruise missiles into Afghanistan. The British mainly struck at targets in Kandahar, where the Taliban headquarters, the airport, and al-Qaeda training camps near the airport were reported to have been hit.

Over the next few days Karzai decided to leave for Uruzgan.[59] People were left behind in Quetta with no idea what was going on. Karzai informed one reporter he was going to Karachi. He told another he was going to Rome. Both journalists were eager to get to southern Afghanistan where the action was, but neither the Taliban nor Pakistan wanted anyone snooping around, and weren't handing out visas. Reporters were active in the north, where they could embed with Northern Alliance troops headed for Kabul, but were totally absent from southern and eastern Afghanistan. US president George Bush had stated that the war on terror would sometimes be fought in secret. Far from the limelight.

Karzai's departure had been thoroughly prepared. A few weeks earlier Karzai had suddenly asked one of Shah's colleagues – a man called Haji Mund, or "The Quiet One" – to grow his beard.[60] This had surprised Haji Mund. The Taliban were plentiful in Quetta, but they were nowhere near as powerful as they were in his homeland Afghanistan, where the beard had to be a fist's length. And now the modern Karzai had demanded that he grow his beard. Just as remarkable was that Karzai himself had sported a short beard for the past two years.

In the evening Haji Mund contacted his friends and gave a confused account of what had happened that afternoon. "What do you men make of it?" he asked. He had sensed for a while that something big was brewing. Messengers were sent from Karzai's villa to southern Afghanistan to get in touch with several of the leader's loyal friends. There was a small group from every province. He had not been aware that Karzai was busy preparing to enter Afghanistan himself, not even when Karzai had instructed him to take three satellite phones to Kandahar. It was obvious to him that Karzai wished to call the recipients of the phones, but what would they discuss?

At the end of September Haji Mund delivered the first phone to a leader who supported the Taliban: Mullah Naqibullah. He was an important figure in the northern part of Kandahar province and had good connections with the Taliban. Haji Mund knew him well because he had been Karzai's guest on a regular basis. It was believed that he secretly kept Karzai up to date about the Taliban's plans. Mullah Naqibullah had had a typically opportunistic Afghan career. He supported the Afghan communists, then fought against the Soviets. Afterwards he was appointed to leadership post within the new Afghan administration led by the Northern Alliance. He then switched sides again when the Taliban took over. In recent years Karzai had frequently tried to win Naqibullah's allegiance, even arranging a visa to Europe for him so he could attend a conference on Afghanistan. Only after 9/11 did Karzai have some success with Naqibullah, which was why the prominent leader accepted the telephone. Naqibullah would soon play a crucial role in the surrender of the Taliban to Karzai. The son of Mullah Naqibullah said that Karzai had called Naqibullah immediately after he got the sat phone. "He said to my father: tell the Taliban not to fight, they are finished. From that early moment, my father kept on telling the Taliban not to fight and that it was over."[61]

In early October Karzai was still misleading Haji Mund. He told him he intended to go to Karachi. Haji Mund thought it was an excellent idea. Quetta wasn't getting any safer. A few days earlier, Karzai had asked him to purchase additional satellite phones and walkie-talkies, but the market in the town centre was a shambles. It was the Taliban's doing, probably encouraged by the Pakistani secret service. They had moved en masse on the bazaar. Nothing was left standing of the booths, the checkpoints, the police station and the surrounding buildings. Everything had been set afire, stoned, or riddled with bullets. Haji Mund was able to ask one of the last remaining vendors what had happened. "Go away," the man had said. "It's not safe here." Karzai understood the situation. "We will leave here soon," he promised. "Make sure everyone's prepared. Invite your families. Invite Shah's family, too. He may be in Uruzgan, but we have to be prepared to leave for Karachi."

Once Operation Enduring Freedom began on October 7, Karzai's *kota* began filling up. Around midnight those present heard his plan to go to Uruzgan. Among them was Ahmad Wali, Karzai's half-brother. He had known, thanks to exchanges with the CIA agent Graig that the American attacks would happen, but his half-brother Hamid's announcement came as a complete surprise.[62]

Ahmad Wali was apprehensive. What was going to happen to Hamid in Uruzgan, he wondered. Would the doors of the *kalas* in Uruzgan be opened to him? Would the people let him in? Ahmad Wali knew it was a Pashtun custom to receive travellers hospitably, particularly in times of trouble. But he was also aware that letting Karzai in brought with it great risk and that this often weighed heavier than unwritten, centuries-old rules. The men he visited would want to know how strong he was, how many men supported him. If they thought he was too weak, the likelihood that they would open their houses to him would be minimal. It would be much easier for the Uruzganis to let him in if, for instance, he had a team of American soldiers with him or if he had American air cover. Ahmad Wali believed that his half-brother was placing himself in danger. But Hamid would hear none of it.

In the following days Karzai stopped by his wife's residence to pick up some essentials. He had only accepted an arranged marriage at age forty, and hadn't known her all that long. He didn't tell her the truth. The fear of betrayal was so great that he couldn't confide in her, Karzai said in an interview. He told her he needed to attend a funeral near the Afghan border. She was surprised when Karzai asked her for a toothbrush and some clean clothes. "What do you need those for if you're only going to pay your respects to the family?" Karzai told his wife that this was no time for explanations. When she handed him the items he told her, "If you don't hear from me within a few weeks, I will be dead." He slammed the door behind him as he left.

When Karzai's jeep sped away from Quetta, it was full of trusted fellow tribesmen. In the front were Karzai's younger cousin and the driver. Karzai himself was in the back, tucked between two bodyguards—colleagues of Shah. The men had not yet been told what their real destination was. "We are going to a funeral in Chaman," Karzai said curtly. When the car drove away, Ahmad Wali silently wept. This could be the last time he would see Hamid, he realised. On his street his departure was immediately noticed. "Where are they going?" the neighbours asked Ahmad Wali. Although he cried when the men left, he now put on a brave face, "He is going to Islamabad," he told them.

The men headed in the direction of the border crossing near the Pakistani city of Chaman, a non-stop drive that would take the rest of the afternoon. But they weren't going to a funeral. Karzai thought they could stay the night there with a relative, also a Popolzai. He would actually have preferred not to use this road to enter the area. Afghans have a habit of taking the long route if they have good connections along the way – it's safer. Karzai knew a Pakistani elder who lived along a less busy road, but he had told Karzai he would have to wait at least two more days before leaving. This was too long for his liking. He couldn't stay in Pakistan any longer. The pressure was mounting— he felt he had to leave. Karzai had kept silent about it for so long already, so he took the main road. Karzai recalls that the trip had already been postponed because he had also been approached by the Pakistani administration. They wished to talk to him in Islamabad about Afghanistan's future. Karzai didn't completely trust the request because Pakistan had always supported the Taliban. "I needed time to think about it. In the end I cancelled." A high official of the Pakistan Military Intelligence in Quetta remembers Karzai visited him, and requested a safe passage to the border. The high official says he arranged accordingly, and asked help from an influential elder of the Ajakzai-tribe.[63]

The next day, in the busy border town of Chaman, it became clear what Karzai's next step would be. He intended to cross the border on a motorcycle.[64] He asked Haji Mund to buy two motorcycles at the market, but their host intervened. He was disturbed by the idea of Hamid crossing the border. Refugees had started to stream en masse from Afghanistan toward Chaman. For the host this was an indication of how serious the situation was in Afghanistan. Cruise missiles and bombs were dropping all over the place and Karzai shouldn't go there. Without telling Karzai, he sent Haji Mund back to Quetta. "Get the motorcycles there if you must," he told him, followed by a lie: "They aren't for sale in Chaman." With Haji Mund out of the way, it was possible that Karzai would now drop his ridiculous plan. But when Karzai discovered that his man had left Chaman, he was angry. "I can't stay here too long," he yelled at his host. "People will see me. I need to cross the border."

Karzai turned to his nephew Ahmed. "You must go to the market instead. You can get a motorcycle here in Chaman, can't you?" Ahmed laughed. "Of course. You can even buy second hand planes here." When he returned with two motorcycles and spare parts, Karzai asked him if the road to the border was safe. Ahmed offered to go ahead and scout out the route.

That afternoon, after the inspection, Karzai's group left on the two motorcycles. Haji Mund was still on his way to Quetta. The host's son had joined the group, crossing the border with Karzai's remaining bodyguard, followed a few minutes later by Karzai's nephew and Karzai himself. The group had divided up the dollars and rupees into small packages. The two satellite phones were stashed at the bottom of a bag. They had nothing else with them. At Ahmed's request, Karzai wore a turban, something he rarely did. This way they looked like regular Afghans traveling by motorcycle—a common sight in Afghanistan. It was imperative that Karzai be taken to Uruzgan as inconspicuously as possible.

Crossing the border between Pakistan and Afghanistan is not difficult. The Durand Line – a line drawn on the map by the British in the nineteenth century – has never been formally recognised by the Pashtun people on either side of it. Karzai's convoy crossed at prayer time, when border control officials had all gone to the mosque. They weren't asked for passports.

Karzai and his nephew allowed themselves to be swept along by the busy traffic flow on the long road to Kandahar city. Capture by the Taliban could mean the end of their expedition, and even wors, their death. But according to the intelligence of Pakistan Karzai had arranged support. "One of his aids along the road to Kandahar knew about the plan. His nick name was Gran Feda and he was able to help."[65] They stopped just outside Kandahar—not because the Taliban had stopped them, but because of a flat tire that occurred when Ahmed accidentally drove over a big stone. It was an anxious moment for the two men. "What now? What do we do? What do you suggest?" Karzai asked Ahmed. "The spare parts are on the bike ahead of us," he replied. Karzai was frustrated and wondered how long they would be delayed. Luckily the men on the other motorcycle looked back. So as not to lose any more time, they exchanged bikes and Karzai and his nephew continued, right across southern Afghanistan, past Taliban check-points, and counter to the flow of displaced people. No one paid attention to them. The next safe house would be in Shorandam, with another of Karzai's relatives.

* * *

WHEN I SAT across from Karzai in his palace in Kabul eight years later, we talked at length about his motorcycle trip. It was about five in the afternoon when I had managed to get a second interview with the President. During the first interview we had breakfast. This time we sat in a small side room, on brown leather Chesterfield-style chairs. There was a bowl of chocolates on the glass coffee table, along with a cup of tea for Karzai and coffee for me. When we got to the moment that he described asking for lodgings at the house in Shorandam, it was quiet. He put his hands on the armrests and thought for a long time.

When he resumed the narrative, he took us to the courtyard of the *kala* where he stayed that night. "The first bombs had fallen in Kandahar and many people were fleeing. My relative was home alone. He said absolutely nothing. Then I saw two small children in the evening silence, walking around on the flat roofs of the buildings. They brought me tea and ran off again. I asked what was going on. "Where are all the villagers? It's so empty here." My host answered: "We're all afraid. American airstrikes are taking place all over and the Taliban are numerous. We could be killed. And so could those children."

Karzai was silent again. He hunched forward as if suddenly feeling the heavy burden on his shoulders, and began to cry softly.

He stares ahead with moist brown eyes. It had been quiet for a long time. He grabbed a white handkerchief and carefully dabbed his eyes. He almost whispered: "Those children weren't even scared. They were my nephews. I even asked my host, 'Why aren't they scared?'"

I asked Karzai what got to him the most. "I felt guilty in that house—terribly guilty—because of those little children. I was afraid they would be murdered because of my presence. Because the Taliban wanted to get me."

* * *

AFTER STAYING THE night in Shorandam, they moved to the next safe house, in Kandahar city. It was deserted. The family had locked the door and fled the airstrikes. The Taliban's epicentre was not far from there, maybe a twenty-minute drive. Mullah Omar, the enigmatic Taliban ruler, had spoken out. His headquarters in Kandahar city were hit by an airstrike, but he seemed unharmed. Via the BBC, he responded furiously to the American attack and he called Afghans who supported it heathens and enemies of Islam. The Americans were aware that many Afghans shared his views. In the media they repeated over and over that they didn't intend to wage a war on Islam or on Muslims, but against terrorists and those who were harbouring them. The Americans' expectation that the Taliban would surrender en masse after the first airstrikes had been shattered. Most of them opted to wait and see if the Americans were serious before taking sides.

Because this was an emergency, Karzai's men wanted to break down the door of the safe house. It was a relative's home and they could explain their actions later. Karzai objected. "There will be no breaking down anything here," he said sternly. In the end, his nephew went around back and climbed over the mud brick wall. He managed to open the door from the inside.

Once they were in, Karzai began frantically making phone calls.[66] The first conversations were in English and his men didn't understand. Who he was talking to and what he said exactly remained a mystery to them, but it was obvious that Karzai was giving foreigners detailed information about his plans. Karzai not only called foreigners, but also the former Afghan king, who was in Rome. He didn't get him on the phone—he spoke instead to the king's cabinet chief. "I am in Afghanistan," said Karzai and then he broke off the connection to save the phone's battery. The cabinet chief at the other end wasn't surprised. He had known of Karzai's plan to go in. The king was notified.

* * *

IN THE MEANTIME Haji Mund had returned from Quetta and was rejoining the group. Karzai gave him no opportunity to recover. He needed to scout out the 75 mile long road from Kandahar city to Tarin Kot, the capital of Uruzgan. Where were the checkpoints? Would Taliban groups along the way be a problem? Karzai wanted to know it all before moving on to his final destination. Haji Mund also had to pick up Karzai's trusted primary bodyguard, Mohammed Shah. Karzai wanted him close during the long and treacherous journey.

Haji Mund encountered few problems on his scouting mission and he arrived safely at Abdul Ghani's home in Kot Wal village, north of Tarin Kot, where Shah had been staying for the past week.

When Haji Mund explained what was going on, Shah shook his head. "So he did it anyway, he went in," he said. Shah immediately turned on the phone, which required placing the receiver in the windowsill so that it can pick up the satellite signal. Then Shah called Karzai: "I'm staying here in Tarin Kot with people who have already done a lot for us and who will support us. But some of the elders refuse to help." Again Shah impressed upon Karzai that he would do better to stay away from Uruzgan. Karzai wouldn't hear of it telling Shah he was already in Kandahar city and that his warnings were pointless. So Shah promptly rushed to Kandahar city with Haji Mund, still hoping to talk Karzai out of it. As Karzai's principal bodyguard he felt responsible. He believed that he was more capable of judging the danger than was Karzai. Once in the city, he talked to him again, sternly. "What are you doing here? Why didn't you say anything? There are people ready in Uruzgan, but you shouldn't go there yourself. It's too dangerous." When Karzai refused to listen, he tried a different tack. "If you die, the whole country is in trouble. If I die, only my family will miss me. I will go to Uruzgan. Take good care of my little boy if I'm gone." But even that didn't sway Karzai. He sent Shah to the center of Kandahar to rent a car.

The rented station wagon was full, and Haji Mund had to sit in the trunk. They drove toward Uruzgan in the dusky late afternoon, along a bumpy road riddled with potholes and through the verdant Shah Wali Kot district, a relatively safe area for Karzai because many fellow tribesmen lived there. But it wasn't completely without danger. Suddenly they came upon a checkpoint. A man in a long *shalwar qamees* stood in the middle of the road. He flagged down the old Corolla, brandishing his Kalashnikov. Seeing other Taliban ahead, they complied. Everyone got out except Karzai. "Where are you going?" the Taliban guard asked threateningly. "It's late." Shah took the lead. He mumbled something about fleeing, like everyone else. He hoped to get it over with quickly this way, but it wasn't that easy. "What's this? Open it up," the man indicated between Karzai's legs with the beam of his flashlight—the bag with the telephones. Karzai refused. The men began to panic. Karzai had been so careful prior to this, never daring to travel with the satellite telephones, and now he had two with him. The men concluded silently that they had miscalculated.

The Taliban guard ordered Karzai to get out of the vehicle and bring the bag with him, but Shah jumped in. When he stood before the man, he said, "No, just leave it. It's not a weapon, it's not a bomb, it's only a box with women's cosmetics." Men weren't allowed to look at women's items, except those that belonged to their own wives. This was the rule, but it was also an excuse that has been used all too often. It was also after nine o'clock and the evening curfew was in effect, so the men weren't even supposed to be on the road. At first the Taliban guard was friendly toward the little group: "Bandits are committing robberies a few miles further on, near Tarin Kot," he warned. "It's my duty to stop you." But Shah still had to open the bag. The guard tapped the box with his Kalashnikov. "Open up!" he yelled.

Karzai could only wonder whether this was the end for him. He tensed up. The guard still insisted. "It's up to you," he told Shah. "You can't drive on unless you show it to me." Shah argued with him, but then the guard told him they would go to his superior. He pointed upward, to the mountain, to another checkpoint, a much bigger one. This was where the commanders were. Karzai didn't go because he couldn't afford to be recognised.

In the lion's den all eyes were on Shah. But he refused to be intimidated. The Taliban guard told his commander: "This gentleman refuses to open his bag." The commander smiled malevolently. "Why do you play with the Taliban?

It's better that you don't, eh?" Shah started talking as if his life depended upon it. One moment he was crying, the next he was yelling: "I have a problem. I'm on my way to my family in Tarin Kot. One of them was murdered, another wounded. We have been to a hospital in Pakistan and I don't know who is feeding my family in Tarin Kot." And so he went on, using one excuse after another. Then it occurred to Shah to ask them if they even knew what was going on in Kandahar. Apparently the men, from a different province, hadn't been there for a while. When Shah told them about the air strikes they gradually began to believe him. In the end Karzai and his entourage were allowed to drive on. A flashlight signalled down the mountain. It flickers three times, the signal that they could proceed.

Late in the evening the men had to approach the house of a sympathetic imam as quietly as possible. He was one of the men who had been invited to Quetta. Around 11 p.m. they left the station wagon on the main road and walk to Gogarak village. It was still too dangerous, so they stayed away from the nearby capital Tarin Kot. Along the way they briefly lost Karzai. While approaching the walled *kala* in the dark, he had failed to notice a small irrigation ditch. He tripped and fell in. The men were alarmed, but before they knew it he had reappeared. "Everything's fine," he said, his clothes dripping with water.

SEVEN

Doubles in Durji: The First Confrontation With the Taliban

T HE IMAM HAD been at mosque when Said came calling. "Karzai is on his way to your house," the messenger whispered to him. "He'll be there any minute." The imam was taken completely by surprise. He quickly finished his prayers and hurried back to his kala, where he found Karzai waiting. He fretted that he wouldn't be able to prepare a decent meal at this hour. Meat couldn't be bought until the following morning, and he had his women make something simple with eggs and beans for his important guest. After they ate Karzai told the imam his intentions for Uruzgan. "The West no longer wants the Taliban," he told him. It was a familiar refrain, and his men had heard it all before, in Quetta. Operating from the imam's kala, Karzai mustered small groups of men together to discuss their plans. Who would join them and who wouldn't? Who would go to which elder to announce Karzai's plans?

Karzai's host was close to the enemy. His mosque was also a madrassa where he gave daily lessons to students of the Koran. "I knew those men, those Taliban. And I also realised how difficult it would be for Karzai," the imam later told me. He pointed out to Karzai that the Taliban office was a stone's throw from his house. They didn't have much space to manoeuvre. How long will all this take, the imam wondered, although he didn't dare ask it out loud. Karzai had not mentioned how long he planned to stay, and this annoyed him. As long as Karzai was under his roof, he had to keep his regular guests out. How long could he keep it up without raising suspicion? What would he do tomorrow? And the day after that? Whatever happened, the imam would go to work as usual, that much was certain. In the mosque he would pretend he knew nothing and would act ordinary. He would pretend Karzai didn't even exist. And if visitors arrived for Karzai, they would not be welcome at his front door; he would send them quick around the back of the kala, where they would have to climb the wall of the compound to gain entry.

The first few days very little happened. Whether Karzai was deliberately waiting to take action wasn't clear. The men accompanying him claimed he wanted to rest first. Karzai even found the time to go jogging every now and then. He didn't run in the village streets—it was too dangerous. He stayed within the *kala* walls and ran laps within its confines.

In the meantime Said was sent out again, this time to notify another Popolzai leader, Mualim Rahmatullah, from eastern Tarin Kot, of Karzai's arrival. Rahmatullah was, like Karzai's other allies, similarly cautious. For years he had been a loyal fellow tribesman, and he often went to see Karzai in Quetta. When Karzai's staunchest ally, Jan Mohammed, went to prison, Rahmatullah gradually took his place. But the big Afghan with the loud laugh and large belly hesitated when he learned that Karzai was in the region. Come with me to Karzai, Said told him from the doorway to Rahmatullah's house. The door was slammed shut in his face. "We have no weapons, everything has been taken," he hissed. Rahmatullah had started his career as a schoolteacher, but when the Soviets arrived in 1979 he left the classroom to fight them, becoming a military commander. When the Taliban were in power he had been placed under house arrest because of a dispute with a governor. He was trapped. He wasn't even allowed to show his face in the centre of Tarin Kot.

In the end Said persuaded him. With a large cotton shawl over his turban, covering his face so he would not be recognised, Rahmatullah climbed onto the back of the motorcycle. Said didn't turn on the headlight. At this late hour they would have to avoid attracting Taliban attention. Karzai's messenger took the Popolzai leader from eastern Tarin Kot through the steppe region, past the river with its green banks, to the north of the provincial capital.

With that, the number of Popolzai deciding to support Karzai increased slowly but surely. But it wasn't enough, and Karzai asked for additional support from other tribes in Uruzgan. His first success was with the Hazara from the northern-most point of Uruzgan province. They constitute about ten percent of Uruzgan's population. Many Hazaras didn't think too highly of the Taliban. One of the local Hazara leaders, Khalili, was in the resistance and worked closely with Jan Mohammed and Karzai. They frequently came up with plans for operations against the Taliban. The

Taliban in Uruzgan generally left Hazara territory alone and the Hazara themselves were able to plan an uprising unnoticed. There had even been talk of an emergency hospital for the wounded that would be arriving from the front. Khalili felt it was too dangerous to travel to Tarin Kot himself, but he sent a messenger to offer as much support as might be needed. "I want to fight on your side," he informed Karzai.

Having Hazara support was a big step, but Pashtun support was still more important, since they made up the rest of Uruzgan's population. But it would have been a mistake to view the Pashtuns as one people. Karzai understood only too well that divisions within the tribes could work against the big picture and that it was therefore crucial he knew precisely who was who. Only then would he be able to pull it off.

The first rough division within the Pashtun was that between the Durrani and the Ghilzai, who both claimed to have had a central role in the establishment of Afghanistan as a nation. Karzai belonged to the first group. They were by far and away the majority Pashtun group in Uruzgan, as well as in Kandahar Province, and are descendants of the first emir of Afghanistan, Ahmad Shah Abdali, later known as Ahmad Shah Durrani. The men Karzai had gathered together in Tarin Kot were also Durrani. They see themselves in dynastic terms because they have provided almost all the leaders of Afghanistan since the seventeenth century, and have had the most important positions within the government for as long as anyone could remember.

In general the Durrani look down on the Ghilzai, the

other main Pashtun tribe. To the Durrani, Ghilzai literally translates to something like "mountain man," but also "thief" or "criminal." Others call them nomads or bums. The Ghilzai themselves have a different view, claiming credit for the establishment of Afghanistan. It's said that the Ghilzai drove out the Persians in the sixteenth century, under the leadership of Mirwais Khan Hotak. Under his rule many Durrani from the south were driven out of the area to western Afghanistan. With the emergence of Ahmad Shah Abdali half a century later, the roles were reversed and it was the Ghilzai who had to flee. However, not all the Durrani shared control. Authority was mainly held by the Zirak, which represents the most important Durrani tribes. Like the Ghilzai, the other important sub tribe of the Durranis – Panjpai – are often viewed by the Zirak as thieves and bums. So it's no surprise that throughout Afghan history the Panjpai have often fought alongside the Ghilzai against the Zirak.

Although Karzai usually prefers to emphasise that all Afghans are one people, he enjoyed relating the myths about his Popolzai tribe and their patriarch Zirak. Zirak had three sons, the old story goes. Barak was the eldest, then Aloko and Popal. According to the myth, when Zirak was 100 and could barely walk, he asked his three sons to help him go to Kandahar. In Karzai's version the first two refused, but Popal lifted his father onto a camel and accompanied him to the ancient city. Later, when Zirak was 120, Popal was rewarded and succeeded his father. Needless to say, Karzai is one of the "sons of Popal," or Popolzai.[67]

When the Taliban took control in 1994, the often marginalised Ghilzai and Panjpai tribes enjoyed, for the first time in centuries, renewed authority and influence in Kandahar. Not all the Ghilzai are Taliban, even though it has often been perceived this way in the West. For instance, through his father, Karzai knew the prominent Ghilzai Hashem Khan, who opposed the Taliban and lost his position of authority within his sub-tribe because of it. An opposing tribal member chose to support the Taliban, thus marginalising Khan. While the Taliban were in power he sat it out in his *kala*, waiting for better times. When he heard in October 2001 that the Popolzai Hamid Karzai had arrived in Uruzgan, he immediately went to him and offered his help. Hashem Khan claimed he could bring the Ghilzai in Tarin Kot over to Karzai's side, as well as his relatives in two other districts of Uruzgan. Like many Ghilzai, these families had sided with the Taliban, but, Khan claimed he could persuade them, a feat that Karzai, a Popolzai, would not be able to achieve on his own. Karzai was pleased with the support and gave Khan all the discretionary power he needed. "Do what you have to," Karzai said, giving him 200,000 Pakistani rupees (then about US$3200). Mualim Rahmatullah resented the fact that Hashem Khan, a Ghilzai, was receiving twice as much as he did, even though he was Popolzai like Karzai. He attempted to appropriate 50,000 rupees of Hashem Khan's money, but to no avail.

*   *   *

IN THE MEANTIME Karzai was growing increasingly exasperated in the imam's *kala* outside Tarin Kot. The batteries for his two satellite telephones were nearly empty, making it harder for him to stay in contact with his allies. In the past two weeks he had ceaselessly called other leaders in Uruzgan, the Northern Alliance, Ismael Khan – who planned to enter Afghanistan from the west any day now – and the Americans. He had smuggled in the two phones, but no extra batteries. The old *kala* hadn't had electricity in years, so recharging was impossible. In desperation he tried to connect the telephone to a car battery, and when this didn't work, he even laid them in the sun, to no avail. "Does anyone have a generator?" Karzai asked. The men surrounding him wondered if he knew where he was. Generators were a rare commodity here, but Karzai had money so he sent someone off to arrange for one.

He also sent Said to Kandahar to pick up two additional telephones. The city had come under increasing attack since the first airstrikes of October 7. Since the Taliban didn't surrender after the first airstrikes, heavier bombers, like the B-52, the B-1, and the B-2 were now being deployed. More of the dull gray AC-130H gunships flew over Kandahar from Pakistan. Around this time the Americans deployed the first ground troops around the city, as part of the short-lived Operation Rhino. At night American commandos attacked the Taliban headquarters and the airport, and then left. The campaign had probably failed.

Brand-new telephones, just delivered by Karzai's half-brother Ahmad Ali, were waiting for Karzai in one of

Karzai's bodyguard's homes. The calls cost US$5 per minute but money was no object because the CIA was paying.[68] Convenient, thought Said, who by now also understood how these things worked.

Despite the distracting trouble with the telephones, Karzai continued his unwavering search for allies among other tribes, like the Barakzai, a Zirak tribe like Karzai's own Popolzai. This wasn't easy in Tarin Kot. Before the Taliban took control, relations within the city were extremely tense. Then-governor Jan Mohammed of the Popolzai was fighting for dominance with the Barakzai. Although it's not certain who started the clash, the Barakzai accused Jan Mohammed of killing a well-known Mullah. A series of murders on both sides followed. Karzai himself was almost a victim when he visited Jan Mohammed in the early 1990s. A Barakzai delegation claiming to want to see Karzai invited him to a meeting near the Central Mosque, where a pistol was promptly shoved in his neck.[69] In the ensuing melee, Jan Mohammed shot the gunman and four other men in broad daylight. There were dead bodies scattered in front of the entrance to the mosque, including that of the governor's driver. Karzai escaped and fled to the house of the police chief Aziz. Although Karzai tried to prevent reprisals against the Barakzai, Jan Mohammed wouldn't listen and a large group of Barakzai were detained. The local Barakzai leader, Rozi Khan, had his revenge by ordering the assassination of Jan Mohammed's brother. For years, enmity between the two leaders remained.

Karzai couldn't count on Rozi Khan in October 2001,

but there were other Barakzai leaders in Tarin Kot, such as Sultan Mohammed and Juma Khan, who had nothing to do with the feud. Both played a significant role in local government prior to the Taliban regime, and Sultan Mohammed had even worked with Jan Mohammed when the latter had been governor. Along with the police chief, Aziz, the three men used to make up the local government of Uruzgan province. With the arrival of the Taliban they lost their positions. Sultan Mohammed fled to Quetta while Juma Khan, by his own account, was imprisoned and tortured. Both of them were hostile toward the Taliban and had sought out Karzai even prior to September 11.

The two elders called on Karzai in the middle of the night. Karzai repeated what he had said so often during the past few weeks, although it had made little impact so far. "The West is fed up with the Taliban," he told them, "and they will be driven out." He also argued that it was specifically the Pashtun who should take action, because now that everything seemed to be shifting in Afghanistan, other groups could profit. Karzai was referring in particular to the Northern Alliance of Uzbeks, Tajik and Hazara mujahideen groups, who, with help from the CIA, were making considerable inroads against the Taliban. The Alliance was steadily moving toward Kabul, but in the south the Pashtun people weren't revolting at all, despite the constant airstrikes on Kandahar city. Karzai realised he was losing time. "We Pashtuns will be in trouble if we do nothing," he argued. "We must defend our position." The two Barakzai sitting opposite him in the *kota* heard Karzai talking and nodded in agreement.

Things still weren't moving fast enough for Karzai. The men in the *kala* mainly argued and bickered and Karzai was contradicted time and again. He was disappointed with the men's ambivalence—they still hesitated to commit. He had been paying them for years and what was he getting in return? Karzai was convinced of the importance of his mission and he didn't understand why the others didn't see the situation as plainly as he did. "I travelled here, all the way from Quetta, and this is all you can offer me?" Said heard him say. Word came of a turncoat in Quetta. The former governor of Kandahar province, Gul Agha Sherzai, who was also set aside by the Taliban and ready to enter Afghanistan via Quetta with suitcases full of money, had bowed out, claiming that he didn't believe Karzai was already in Uruzgan. Now that the cards were being reshuffled in Afghanistan he had other plans, and Karzai lost an ally for good.

After a few days Karzai's group moved to the home of Abdul Ghani Mama in Kot Wal. The situation was too dangerous for them to stay in one place for very long. Karzai would have preferred to go by car, but the men disagreed. He would have to walk, and it was too danger-ous for the group to be on the move in daylight. They waited until nightfall to set out. Said roared past the group on his motorcycle, moving ahead to inspect the new place before the rest of the party arrived. Afterward he moved on to Deh Rawud, where there were a few men who had visited Karzai in Quetta. They quickly joined the group.

Even though the company around Karzai was taking a wait-and-see approach, there were still mouths that had to be fed. If there was no food in the *kota*, the warriors would leave. The women in the *kala* were barely able to keep up, and Karzai asked his half-brother Ahmad Wali in Quetta for help. Karzai bought all sorts of things to make them comfortable, and even had cars sent, as well as motorcycles and generators. The constant stream of CIA dollars and rupees – sometimes 80,000 dollars, sometimes 100,000 dollars—ensured that there was no shortage of money.[70] While Karzai was in Uruzgan, Ahmad Wali went back and forth between Quetta and the CIA office in Islamabad to ensure Karzai had everything he needed. He made secret arrangements with agents in Islamabad, sometimes in an underground parking garage, sometimes waiting inconspicuously in his car on a busy street, waiting for another car to pull up alongside to hand a bag of telephones and money through the window. During the first weeks of Karzai's mission Ahmad Wali was one of the few in Quetta who knew everything that was going on in Uruzgan, but he said nothing. When reporters called him to ask where his half-brother was, he mentioned Islamabad or Karachi, never Uruzgan. Karzai had to have enough reliable allies in Uruzgan before his brother could reveal anything.

Karzai was now on Washington's radar, though.[71] His name featured in CIA director George Tenet's briefing to President George Bush and Secretary of Defense Donald Rumsfeld. They were anxious about the situation in southern Afghanistan. While the Northern Alliance was moving rapidly toward Kabul, Kandahar was still quiet. Rumsfeld wondered what the people in the south were waiting for. Tenet mentioned Karzai, portraying him as a relatively insignificant Pashtun leader. A clean-cut man of forty-four, fluent in English, somewhere near Tarin Kot. A perfect spot for a CIA team to fly in.

At this point Karzai's base in Uruzgan was still far from solid. Growing numbers of men were being brought in from Quetta, including some relatives. But tensions were stoked when his men discovered that Karzai had forgotten to have the mission blessed by an important religious leader. There was no *fatwa*, the religious decree he would need for his plans to be considered legitimate. He had been told before September 11 that he needed a mullah's approval for his opposition activities. Then he had arranged it, but not now, and a hasty search ensued for a Mullah prepared to legitimise the uprising in Uruzgan. A religious leader from Quetta finally issued a *fatwa*, ensuring Karzai's mission could continue.

Despite the *fatwa*, Karzai could see for himself that the morale of his men wasn't getting any better. They were increasingly skeptical that they could take Karzai at his word. "If the Americans support you," they challenged him, "then prove it—have a bomb dropped on Tarin Kot. Then we will take the town and definitely bring an end to the Taliban regime." For Karzai, this was deeply disturbing. "How dare you ask for such a thing?" he responded. "How can I ask America to bomb my Afghanistan? Innocent civilians live there, too." His fighters, willing to give their own lives for Karzai, were unsympathetic. They had been spinning their wheels for a while, and they needed guarantees. The fighters followed with another request: "Then have a bomb dropped outside the city. Have it dropped in the desert—give us a sign." Karzai knew he could always ask for American assistance, but he was adamant.[72] Bombing was a step too far. He finally met the men halfway by promising them a weapons drop. A few of them had secretly brought along a Kalashnikov or some other weapon, but it wasn't enough. One of the men knew of a place where weapons could be gathered. They would have to go into the mountains, where helicopters or other aircraft could deliver their cargo reasonably undisturbed.

The tension in Karzai's group rose when his presence in the province was leaked. "The Taliban mayor of Tarin Kot knows," one of them yelled. It was unclear who had fed the information to him. Karzai's Popolzai assumed it was Khodai Nazar, a well-known leader of the rival Noorzai tribe in western Uruzgan. He had visited Karzai's *kota* and had even received money in exchange for his support, but when he left, closing the door behind him, he disappeared. It was a blow for Karzai, who no longer knew if he could trust his own men, worrying that if things kept going this way they could end up shifting their allegiance to the Taliban. Or worse, they could hand him over.

*   *   *

THE NEXT DAY they heard loud explosions. Karzai called his host to the window. "Look and see what's happening there," Karzai said. Some in the *kala* thought planes were firing rockets in retaliation for being shot at themselves. Others didn't see any aircraft—they thought the rockets were coming from the sea. Everyone in the *kala* was flabbergasted, none more so than Karzai. When he saw the smoke plumes above Tarin Kot, he angrily reached for a telephone. The ensuing conversation was in English. "Why was I not informed about this attack?" he asked. "You're bombing regular civilians and it's also terribly close to my safe house. Why on earth are you launching rockets?"

It was October 20, 2001. Tarin Kot was attacked twice, striking the police station and the Taliban military headquarters.[73] Karzai was fuming. It was as if the Americans had completely forgotten about him, or didn't even know about his mission. He didn't want bloodshed. Rockets wouldn't just hit the Taliban, they would also hit innocent civilians. He feared the families of the dead civilians would turn on the source of the attacks rather than the Taliban, and the last thing he needed was angry families. He had to be able to move quietly from *kota* to *kota*, with only a few armed men for protection. He mainly wanted to talk, negotiate, and bribe if necessary. He was a politician, a former diplomat, trying to make his way peacefully through a tribal landscape. He believed that most Afghans who supported the Taliban weren't religious fanatics or terrorists. They were just opportunists who had made the wrong choice.

The attack had seriously shaken the usually-quiet Tarin Kot. Curious men climbed onto the roofs of their *kalas* and loudly asked one another what had happened. They watched the tall smoke plumes rising above the city. Around them everyone was out and about. On any other day, families would have been concealed behind the tall walls of their *kalas* and street life would have been practically non-existent. Now, everyone was outside. Most people had no idea what was going on. Taliban were fleeing the city. Whole groups of citizens were on the move, searching for refuge in the suburbs or high in the mountains. Regular criminals and prisoners detained by the religious police had managed to escape from the local jail.

By the following day Karzai's fears had been substantiated. The Taliban weren't the only ones hit. With the American war just a few weeks old, Karzai could already see that innocent civilians had become victims.

After the rocket attack there was initially a celebratory mood in the old *kala* of Aziz, the former Uruzgan police chief. His sons were eating in the light blue *kota* when they heard the whizzing sound of the rockets and the loud thud of their impact. Dogs ran in a panic toward Aziz's sons, but were shooed away. The boys ran to the roof. Could this be an attack on the Taliban? They had been aware for a few days that something was brewing in the city. A few days ago their father was invited to join his friend Hamid Karzai, who as far as they knew lived in Quetta, but was now apparently in Tarin Kot. Their father hadn't said much about it.

Aziz's sons were curious. The family had suffered much under the Taliban regime. Their father even fled for a year, after he was repeatedly threatened by a rival cousin who had joined the Taliban. Since his return he had waited quietly to see what would happen with the Taliban. The thunder of the airstrikes could very well be another chance, his sons thought. Maybe Karzai would topple the regime and make their father powerful again, like he was before the

Taliban. It would be as if there had never been any Taliban.

The next morning little of the excitement remained. After the rocket attacks the Americans tried to keep track of the fleeing Taliban from the air, but they couldn't discern between the Taliban and regular civilians. Relatives of Aziz tried to leave Tarin Kot on a tractor but the Americans were faster. A rocket struck the middle of the group, not far outside of town. Aziz lost nine relatives and his daughter was wounded. The day before, Aziz had been celebrating a wedding in a mountain village. When he heard the rockets he returned as quickly as he could. A family meeting was held in his *kota* and they decided to bury all nine bodies together. Later, they would bury them all in separate graves. For the moment Aziz wanted no further involvement in Karzai's activities.

After the attacks, nothing seemed to be a secret any longer in Tarin Kot. More and more people were aware that Karzai was in the vicinity. The pressure on his *kala* was mounting. The Taliban or members of rival families were trying to get close. They sent men who were well-known to Karzai's group to collect information, hoping to kill or stop Karzai. But hardly any succeeded. Often they didn't even make it to the front door, protected not only by Karzai's host, but by families in the nearby *kalas*, who kept a close look out as well.

More bad news arrived over the following days while Karzai was still busy arranging the American weapons drop. The former police chief Aziz was the first to hear it over the radio while in a taxi on his way back from Quetta, where he had taken his wounded daughter to a hospital. A Taliban spokesman triumphantly announced that Abdul Haq had been executed. Haq was the warlord who entered Afghanistan in the east, accompanied by men from his tribe. But after only three days he walked into a Taliban trap. He was interrogated, convicted of espionage, and executed by a firing squad. The rest of his group was hanged shortly afterwards. Haq's death was a hard blow to Karzai's men. He was a renowned warlord who had lost a leg in battle against the Soviets – a man, in short, in whom many had great faith. How could he die? How strong were the Taliban?

Aziz was desperate. What was to become of the "educated one" in Uruzgan? A death as gruesome as Haq's most certainly awaited Karzai as well. If even Abdul Haq couldn't stay alive, their own chances for survival seemed slim. Karzai had been in the region for only two weeks and he probably wouldn't last much longer. The horrified Aziz lay flat on the taxi's back seat the entire drive back to Uruzgan, afraid the Taliban might spot him.

When Karzai himself heard the news on the radio a little later, he was livid. He threw his satellite telephone across the small *kota*. "A great hero has died," he said repeatedly. "A great hero is dead." With danger all around him, he stayed in Uruzgan.

* * *

KARZAI INSTRUCTED SAID to recruit new fighters immediately. It didn't matter if they were true allies or simply mercenaries, as long as the *kota* was full. Meanwhile Karzai himself left for two days with a small group to collect promised American weapons cached for them near Durji, a hamlet high in the mountains northwest of Tarin Kot. The hamlet felt like the end of the world, comprised of about ten houses built up against the side of the mountain. It was the ideal spot, miles from civilisation and populated with residents whose support he could rely on. They were members of a loyal Alikozai tribe; several Popolzai from a little further on would be joining them. The men from Durji were regular guests at Karzai's *kala* in Quetta.[74] Before 9/11, Karzai had paid for their hospital visits and small items, and had asked them to encourage other men in their area to drop by.

The trip to Durji was dangerous. The safest route ran through Jan Mohammed's territory, and many of Karzai's men felt that if only he was with them now, everything would be a lot easier. In the village of Talani they heard that the Taliban had been asking about Karzai and his men. Villagers sent a woman to tell the Taliban that Karzai had never been there. As often in Pashtun culture, a female messenger is sent for only very delicate or important issues. Sending your wife or another related female – often carrying a Koran – highlights that the sender takes the issue very seriously. It's also often a last attempt to solve long conflicts. And that's why the Taliban who talked to the female messenger in Talani also believed her instantly: Karzai wasn't there.

Karzai's small caravan eventually made it to its destination. The local Alikozai family had promised that Karzai could safely hide with them. Although their sons worked for the Taliban, nobody told them anything. Karzai went into the mountains to find a good location for the weapons drop. They couldn't afford anything going wrong; it was obvious that the Taliban were hot on their trail. Karzai found a spot—an open plateau outside Durji—and it was imperative that his fighters be picked up from Tarin Kot so they could all return well-armed from the weapons drop. After staying in Durji for two nights, Karzai went back to get the rest of the men, including the newcomers recruited by Said. In the dead of night the now much larger group – about seventy men – moved to the mountains, their presence betrayed only by the few beams of light from their flashlights, dancing ahead of them. They were to pick up the weapons and then return and position themselves near Tarin Kot as quickly as possible.

Some of the warriors who had been with Karzai from the beginning were too old for trekking into the mountains and didn't accompany him to Durji. Karzai's nephew Ahmed also stayed behind. Some suspected he was afraid of being killed like Abdul Haq, but he denied it. Karzai instructed him to go to Quetta to get two cars and another Popolzai fighter by the name of Obaidullah. But Ahmed and Obaidullah knew one another, and were engaged in a longstanding feud; Ahmed refused, and when Karzai wouldn't back down, the man who smuggled Karzai on a motorcycle into Afghanistan left without saying goodbye. Karzai said, 'don't escape', and he said that the trip was 'historical'. "This, what we are doing here will be written in history." But Ahmed couldn't care less about Karzai's plan and left.[75]

In the meantime Said had received Karzai's shopping list of supplies their group would need in the mountains. Seventy blankets, seventy pairs of shoes, six bags of flour, a bag of sugar, tea, a teapot, mugs, and a large pan, essential supplies for the small army currently on its way to Durji. It was quite an undertaking. Said was afraid of attracting attention in the bazaar of Tarin Kot. Blankets were easy to come by, even though they weren't exactly the kind Karzai had asked for. He went further afield for the other items. Outside the town he asked a trusted merchant to help him. "It doesn't matter what it costs," he said, "as long as you get it all together." He gazed up at the towering mountains and wondered what to do. He couldn't get the supplies up there by car—the trails were too steep. How would he get up there with all that equipment? He went to ask the help of a nomad south of Tarin Kot, close to the airfield. It was dark when he arrived at the nomad's tents. "Please, take your camels, take these supplies, and go to the mountains," Said pointed up, to the high mountains, "Please go to Durji," he asked. Then Said returned to Tarin Kot, where he got a call from Karzai. "Come up here," Karzai told him. "The Americans have brought the weapons."

Although the CIA was aware of Karzai's mission, the long expected weapons drop was chaotic.[76] Graig, the American secret agent, called from Islamabad to discuss the details of the delivery. He instructed Karzai to build four fires around the exact spot where he wanted the weapons to be dropped. Karzai's men set to the task, and when they had completed it they saw two aircraft high above the fires. But nothing happened. The pilots observed the situation on the ground and left. Disappointed, the warriors turned to Karzai. "We built the fires, so where are the weapons?" they asked Karzai. Karzai didn't know what to say. The Americans probably wanted to be sure that everything was as Karzai said. He had also seen a white aircraft circling above Tarin Kot. "Are they looking to see if I have enough men?" he wondered. It was two full days before the drop finally happened. Karzai asked his men to build four fires again on November 1st. They heard the approaching aircraft, the rumbling helicopters used no lights, so that the Taliban wouldn't be able detect them. Two to three hundred Kalashnikovs, rocket launchers and ammunition, all bound onto large pallets, fell from the heavens like manna. News of the drop quickly reached the *kalas* of Tarin Kot and Deh Rawud, and dozens of suddenly inspired men made for the mountains.

The following morning the Taliban announced their presence.[77] Two Afghans from Deh Rawud, well known to Karzai, arrived with a letter. One of them was a brother of Karzai's ally Ibrahim. The other was Mullah Mohammed Anwar. Both were Popolzai who had visited Karzai regularly in Quetta. Today they had come as representatives of Mullah Baradar, himself a Popolzai and a powerful Taliban chief from Deh Rawud. The two men announced a large Taliban attack by forces from Kandahar city, probably sent personally by Mullah Omar.

What happened next is unclear. What is known is that

the same evening a large Taliban group moved to the top of the mountain. Estimates of their numbers vary from 50 to 500. Karzai's group was about 150 strong, although by the time the Taliban arrived their numbers had probably dwindled as men fled the Taliban approach. A few witnesses insist that an intense battle ensued and that Karzai's group got away with a large number of weapons. Others claim that there was some fighting but Karzai's group got away easily after he found out from Mullah Baradar that the force was en route. According to most of the men who where there, Mullah Barader's plan must have been to inform Karzai's people about what was supposed to happen. "This was a dance of the inner circle of the Popolzai", Aziz Agha says. "We don't know exactly what happened and if Mullah Baradar was sent by Mullah Omar, but here tribe relations count. Karzai would care more about the death of Berader then mine; I am a good friend, but not a Popolzai." Ibrahim Akhundzada – the brother of one of the messengers – claimed that Mullah Baradar did not save Karzai. "I don't think he wanted to inform Karzai to help him out. He just wanted to give us a choice." Others, like Wali Jan, claimed that Mullah Barader was saving Karzai's life.

The day after the incident in Durji, the Taliban ambassador in Islamabad, Mullah Zaeef, walked triumphantly toward a microphone. To the great chagrin of the Americans, who were present in the same city, he held almost daily press conferences about Taliban victories in the war. A few days earlier he had told the media in Islamabad, in his distinctive high voice, how the Taliban had captured Abdul Haq. Today he had even more great news. The Taliban had put Karzai's group out of business, killing many of them "Twenty-five men were captured," he told his audience, "the first of whom will be hanged in Kandahar today."

EIGHT

Support From the American A-Team

THE RADIO BLARED bad news, disturbing the natural calm of Said's *kala*. Mullah Rasul, a local Taliban representative in Uruzgan, declared that Karzai had been arrested, along with twenty-five others. The radio announcer reported the Taliban had also confiscated 2,000 Kalashnikovs. Said immediately assumed that Karzai had not survived. His mouth felt rough and dry. He was at a loss. With Karzai dead, the men who had thrown in with him were vulnerable and leaderless. Said saw what was coming: the Taliban would be looking for traitors. They would hunt down Karzai's followers, and Said had been one of them. Thoughts of his family played over and over in his mind. Desperate, he mounted his motorcycle and drove to the mountains where the battle had taken place. It was a hopeless act, but he had to see for himself whether or not Karzai had really been killed. He tried calling Karzai's phone en route, but the line was dead.

Karzai's relatives in Quetta were also worried. All the international media were reporting that the Taliban had defeated an insurgent group in southern Afghanistan and that its leader, a man named Karzai, had presumably been killed. They were sceptical, but feared the worst. Foreign journalists who had frequently used Karzai as an interpreter were at a loss. Phone lines buzzed with the news. Was Karzai dead? Was he executed like Haq? Only Ahmad Wali, his half-brother, remained adamant, telling anyone who would listen that Karzai was alive, though no one believed him. "If he survives, his family and supporters say, the prize is big," The New York Times wrote on that day. "He could emerge as the hero of the resistance to the Taliban and as the ruler of considerable swaths of liberated Afghan territory." Ahmed Wali told the media he was still in Uruzgan, and that he had heard his brother saying through a 'frail' satellite phone that he was 'ok' and that he 'continues working' and that he had 'big things to do'.[78] In the meanwhile, an American official told the journalists about Hamid Karzai's supposedly powerful position. "No one should ever, ever underestimate the amount of his authority," the official said.[79]

In a small room at the Shahbaz Air Base in Jacobabad, one of the largest American bases in Pakistan, a twelve-man American Special Forces A-team, Operational Detachment Alpha (ODA) 574, was also listening to the news.[80] They had been flown in to Pakistan via Uzbekistan. ODA 555, 595, and 585 were already active in the north and west. This A-team was under the command of thirty-year-old captain Jason Amerine. From Hawaii, he had pitch-black hair, and his demeanour was composed and serious. His commandos were specialists in unconventional warfare, and their operations in dangerous areas were highly classified. The teams were accustomed to extended missions in hostile territory, with minimal guidance from headquarters. There were two commandos of each specialty in an A-team, so there was always someone to take over if another member of the team went down. Loved ones were never informed about their work, or where they were deployed. In recent years ODA 574 had carried out so many secret missions in war zones that its members were completely in synch with one another. In this new war they answered to the military call-sign Texas 12.

Jason's team had had an uneventful period training local paramilitary units in Kazakhstan. But after 9/11 everything changed. Like most American A-teams spread out across the globe, they were recalled to the States to prepare in secret for unknown future missions. The Pentagon needed them on the bench, ready to be put into play at short notice. The men stayed in Kentucky for about two weeks, where they had to prove themselves in general training. Cut off from all contact with the outside world, they practiced team building, fighting, and requesting air support. The best among them would be the first to go to Afghanistan.

In the end of October ODA 574 was told to prepare for departure. The commander of the 5th Special Forces Group (Airborne) in Fort Campbell considered Amerine's men to be the most capable, even though their highest-ranking officer was merely a captain. They would be the first A-team in Afghanistan. It was the kind of opportunity that every soldier hopes for – a unique opportunity to put into practice everything they'd learned as commandos.

At that point Amerine knew only their destination.

Everything else was uncertain. The Pentagon was still being vague about the deployment of the A-teams. Amerine didn't know when he would deploy, where exactly in Afghanistan he would be sent to, or what he would be doing there. He didn't know much about Afghanistan itself, either, although one look at the map told him it would be a challenge. He would be operating behind enemy lines, waging invisible guerrilla warfare. The mountains would make travel impossible, and the high peaks were a perfect cover for the enemy. Nevertheless Amerine looked forward to it. He had always wanted to join the Green Berets, and looked forward to clandestine operations and engaging the enemy in battle. After the intense training at Fort Campbell, he and his men had a few days to say goodbye to their loved ones. Amerine flew to his parents in Hawaii. "I can't say how long I'll be gone," he said.

On November 2nd, Amerine and his team landed in Jacobabad. He was informed they would be deployed somewhere in southern Afghanistan. He also learned about the Pashtun, the people of the south who produced the Taliban, supported it, and made it great. In their area Amerine had to form a militia of local insurgents willing to confront the Taliban. Amerine didn't have much to go on, since the maps of Afghanistan weren't up to date. Villages were often marked with completely different names. Amerine and his team studied the yellowed sheets in disbelief.

Amerine knew an opposition leader in the south, Hamid Karzai, would probably be willing to work with the

Americans. "But the plan was fluid from the start," Amerine stated. "There had been no plan to infiltrate the Pashtun tribal belt until Abdul Haq and Hamid Karzai told the US they were going in. In each case, they went in unassisted, refusing direct support. For that reason, my mission took place a month later."

The name Hamid Karzai didn't ring a bell, but his background seemed promising for Amerine: headquarters reported that he was from the influential Popolzai tribe and that he'd been leading the opposition in the south for some weeks When Amerine tried to contact Karzai on his satellite telephone, there was no answer. His A-team felt discouraged: Karzai had probably been killed. Amerine slumped back in his chair and placed his hands behind his head. He looked at the rest of his team. We are in Pakistan, he thought, and we still don't know what we're doing here.

* * *

AS THE WORLD speculated about his fate, Karzai was in the mountain hamlet of Durji. Two of his enemies from the large Taliban group in Kandahar were standing before him. Karzai's men had captured them. "What should we do with them?" they asked, indicating the two frightened Taliban prisoners. "What are we going to do?" his men asked again. They were rhetorical questions—of course the answer was to take revenge, to kill them, to slaughter them. But Karzai called them to order. "No killing!" he yelled at his men. "I don't want these men killed." While his men stood in disbelief, Karzai addressed the prisoners in a friendly tone.

"Go home, keep your heads down, and return to work as usual tomorrow," he told them. When the Taliban rose to power in 1994, they did the same thing to some political rivals. First try to get control by being friendly, by convincing the opposition without using violence, and once you have command and you feel confident, then you choose whom to work with. This seemed to be the best way to change the regime in Afghanistan. Karzai gave the two men some money and let them keep their weapons.

After the Taliban attack, Karzai wanted to leave Durji. A new attack was possible and so he planned to go to Char Chino, a district in the western corner of Uruzgan. Although there were few Popolzai there, he still considered it a good base of operations. He counted on support from the local Noorzai chieftain Mohammed Abdul Rahman.

Before he left, Karzai had his spokesman call the BBC in London, announcing that he was still in Uruzgan, fighting for a better Afghanistan.[81] His goal was a semi-democratic meeting – a traditional *loya jirga* – in which everyone could participate. The BBC editor wondered if it was wise for Karzai to let the whole world know that he's still alive and where he is. The Taliban could easily find him. Karzai was firm, intending to make himself heard before leaving for Char Chino. When the news was broadcast, Karzai's relatives and friends were greatly relieved. The media announced that Hamid Karzai was one of the first Afghan resistance leaders operating in Taliban country. On the BBC, an anchorman pointed to Deh Rawud on a large map of Afghanistan, reporting that "This is where Karzai, a former deputy minister of foreign affairs, is supposedly located."

Late that evening, Karzai had one more meal with his men in Durji before they moved on. As always they ate in silence, using their fingers to scoop yellow rice from large platters. Ibrahim, the mountain man who had been with the group since the start, sat beside Karzai under an almond tree and started to talk. He had always believed Karzai would make it to a position of high authority in Kabul. Even though Karzai had said nothing about his ambitions or plans, it was clear he was arranging all sorts of things. But what will happen to me, Ibrahim wondered. What will happen to all of us when this is over? He needed guarantees that they weren't doing it all for nothing. "Let's say we overthrow the Taliban regime and you become minister or president," he asked Karzai. "Will you still remember us?" Karzai was benevolent. "Of course," Karzai responded. "I promise you all that I won't forget you." The men nodded, satisfied. Ibrahim knew they would hold Karzai to his promise. But Karzai immediately questioned Ibrahim as to whether he would accept a government from Kabul ruling his area? Karzai knew central governments in Kabul had never been popular in provinces like Uruzgan and that this wouldn't change overnight. "I will be sure to think of you," he repeated, "however, you must promise me in turn that you will always respect the law."[82]

The morning of their departure Karzai got up early. Before sunrise he went in search of water. He found a creek, and woke the men for the cleansing ritual and morning prayers. It reflected well on Karzai, Ibrahim observed, as they bent their bodies to the west, in prayer toward Mecca.

The two-day journey that ensued, through Char Chino district, was a disaster. Karzai's men thought that he had miscalculated. The people of the region did not support him. Of the thirty-five men who were with him during the weapons drop, he took along only seven, while the rest returned to Tarin Kot. Some of them believed they should be prepared to defend Tarin Kot because Karzai expected the situation to become unstable there. When Karzai and his remaining group arrived in Char Chino, they didn't get very far before the local Taliban recognised them. They then fled to Duawan, a little further north along the river, but they were turned away. For hours they wandered past the dusty villages of this remote part of Uruzgan, with no luck. After having doors slammed in their faces all day, they left the district, exhausted, in the direction of Deh Rawud, where a relative of one of the men let them in. They were given something to eat—a cup of tea and some almonds— before being sent on their way once again. The news of the attack on Karzai in Durji had made everyone uneasy; the whole province was now aware of his presence.

Karzai and his men turned back, heading in the direction of Durji with some supplies. They wandered around the mountains, but found no place to stay. Eventually they stumbled upon an enclosure, a sheep pen of sorts where nomads occasionally kept their animals. The men improvised and made a bed of animal manure to keep their leader somewhat warm. At five in the morning they suddenly heard bells jingling. The men rushed to finish the morning's first prayer session and hid—it could be Taliban. It turned out to be a long camel caravan approaching them. It was a beautiful sight as the sun rose and the first rays of light hit the mountains. For fifteen minutes they lay there. When the procession drew closer, it turned out to be a bride being escorted from Deh Rawud to Tarin Kot. She was getting married in the provincial capital, as if everything was normal.

Along the way they also encountered a nomad, roaming the mountains with his herd, who gave them eggs and tea. Just after they left, the Taliban paid the nomad a visit, but he didn't betray the group. He admitted he saw some strangers, but he pointed the Taliban in the opposite direction. The Taliban beat him and took the money Karzai had given him for his help. Karzai would never forget the nomad and every year he invites him to his presidential palace for Ramadan, where he gives him money.

After two long days of wandering the men began to complain. Life was hard in the mountains; they were short of supplies, the blankets Said ordered in Tarin Kot never reached the group, and a lot of the weapons from the American drop had been stolen or taken by the Taliban. Morale was plummeting, and the men feared the Taliban had simply become too powerful. "If we had our weapons and enough to eat, we could continue," Karzai said to his men. "But this is useless." They decided to call the Americans in Islamabad to be evacuated.[83] Karzai made it clear to the CIA they needed help, and that same night two helicopters arrived with four Americans aboard. While one helicopter hovered overhead, the other landed. For now,

Karzai's uprising, which had lasted one month, had come to an end.

*   *   *

THE CALL TO prayer rang out from the loudspeakers of the mosque in Tarin Kot. The market stall shutters closed, and rows of men moved to the small building with the light blue minaret. It seemed to be a day like any other in the capital of Uruzgan. Said also went to the mosque, although he knew it was unsafe. He was still distraught. What should he do now? Where was Karzai? He decided to go to the mosque to hear if there was any news.

The mullah's whole sermon was about Karzai's men in the mountains. His voice carried across the room. He was angry, and described Karzai and his loyalists as the "the king's group." The listeners needed no explanation. The mullah saw Karzai as a representative of King Zahir Shah, an unbeliever with ties to the heathen West. "And so Karzai is also a puppet for the West," he shouted at the worshippers sitting before him. "These unbelievers must not be allowed to return to their wives—they are not worthy." It was a way of saying: it is ok to kill these men.

A friend saw Said amid the men in the mosque and nodded in recognition. His gesture was one of warning, telling Said to get away as the situation was too dangerous. That night Said hid at a cousin's house. Who could he trust now? Nothing was certain anymore.

Everyone suspected everyone. While Karzai was being taken to safety by the CIA, the Taliban in Tarin Kot took action. Although the Taliban had a list of Karzai supporters, they entered various Popolzai villages and arrested almost every Popolzai. Said was also detained. He was familiar with this group of Taliban, which came from the Mirabad Valley northeast of Tarin Kot. Their leader was Mullah Shafiq, nemesis of the prominent Popolzai Jan Mohammed, who was being held prisoner in Kandahar City. Said was immediately taken to the mosque and put before the Taliban rulers. The situation was made more tense when he saw a familiar face among the Taliban. When their eyes met Said motioned to him to keep his mouth shut so as not to betray him. He gave a false name and for a while the Taliban were confused. "Why are you holding this man?" they shouted. "He's not on the list." Said didn't wait for them to change their minds. He stepped gingerly out of line, grabbed his sandals, and ran off.

*　　*　　*

THAT NIGHT, NOT more then hundred miles to the West, CIA agent Graig disembarked from the helicopter, surrounded by a huge dust cloud.[84] He had just landed on a plateau high in the mountains near Durji. He looked around through night vision goggles, searching for Karzai. He called out his name in the darkness: "Is that you? Mr Karzai, are you there?" When he saw his Afghan friend standing on the rocks, he greeted him enthusiastically with "Your Excellency." Karzai laughed when he heard this. In our interviews, Karzai said he didn't know if Graig was already referring to his future presidency. The former diplomat found the title flattering, though.

Karzai realised the escape from Uruzgan could hurt his image. Afghans might not appreciate that the leader of the uprising had to be saved by the United States. It was also fodder for the formidable Taliban, who, after killing Haq, had now placed Karzai high on their hit list. So in Durji it was immediately agreed that no-one could know about the rescue.[85] Not his friends and certainly not the media. Before they boarded the helicopter they agreed they would not speak of it. Karzai needed to step out of his own uprising unseen. Within four or five hours he was at the American base in Jacobabad, Pakistan.

But the news was partly leaked even before Karzai had set foot on Pakistani soil. US Secretary of Defense Donald Rumsfeld stated at a press conference on November 6 that "we have airlifted him and taken him to Pakistan for consultation." The Americans accompanying Karzai weren't amused.[86] This only made their job more complicated. They tried to counter the breach with the help of Karzai's half-brother Ahmad Wali in Quetta. He spoke to reporters in Quetta, insisting that Rumsfeld had been misinformed. He repeated over and over: "I have just talked to him on the phone and everything is fine. He's still in Uruzgan, that's a fact." He was up against the secretary and reporters didn't know who to believe. There were no reporters in southern Afghanistan and the media were tossed around by the tug of war between Karzai's family and the Pentagon. Years later, when asked about what really happened, Karzai still didn't want to admit that he had been taken to Pakistan by the Americans.[87]

When the CIA helicopters landed at the military base in Jacobabad, Karzai's men expected a hero's welcome. They proudly climbed down in their dusty *shalwar kameeses*. When they entered the bunker compound, still exhausted from the days-long trek across Char Chino district, they were stopped by a small group of clean-cut Western men in civilian clothing. One of them was even wearing a tie—clearly they were CIA, one of the Afghans thought. But the Americans didn't trust Karzai's men, even thought they had kept him alive all this time. They were searched from head to toe, and even their turbans were lifted from their heads. The Afghans couldn't imagine a bigger insult.

Later, inside the concrete building, Karzai tried to explain to the Americans what had happened in Uruzgan. He praised his Afghans repeatedly. But one of them was angry, and with fire in his eyes he stepped forward. "I was with the mujahedeen who fought the jihad," he cried out in Pashto. Karzai translated for the Americans. "Things went wrong in Afghanistan after the king left," he continued. "Since then the Americans have made one mistake after another in this country. First you helped us to drive out the Soviets but then you left our country to Pakistan. That wasn't too smart. Now you have your towers," the man said angrily. The allusion to 9/11 wasn't lost on the CIA men.

The American with the tie spoke, humbly admitting that mistakes were made. "Thank you very much for helping Mr. Karzai," he said.[88] He also thanked them for their insight into what the Americans had done wrong in the past. "But now we want to help," he explained. "We want to overthrow the regime and attack the Taliban from inside the country together with the Pashtun. Then we will completely rebuild the country in six months, a year at the most."

Over the following days the insurgents saw Karzai come and go. He was usually in a small room nearby, sometimes for hours. They spoke English in there. While his men enjoyed the free food and were relaxing, Karzai held meetings. This first week of November was hectic. The northern city of Mazar-e-Sharif had been taken by the Uzbek general Dostum, and western Herat province was in Ismael Khan's hands. Suddenly the mighty Taliban strongholds seemed to be falling like dominoes.

*   *   *

AROUND THIS TIME the American diplomat James Dobbins was appointed Special Representative of the President of the United States for the Afghan Opposition. His task was to unite all groups fighting the Taliban and to form a government acceptable not only to all the Afghan opposition groups but also to Afghanistan's neighbours.

The balding American had never had anything to do with Afghanistan, and he certainly didn't know anyone in Kabul. He had built up a solid portfolio of similar posts in Somalia, Haiti, Bosnia and Kosovo. Now he would concentrate on Afghanistan, supported by a team of experienced Afghanistan experts in the Bush administration. They had been involved in the Afghan war for a while and had made several trips to the region. There didn't seem to be a precise strategy for the future, but it was clear they would rather not see the old king back in control, and unilateral Northern Alliance leadership was no longer an option.

It was only later, Dobbins has since claimed, that he first heard about Karzai.[89] He had been in a meeting with four-star general Tommy Franks, at the U.S. Central Command in Tampa, Florida, the military base where the war in Afghanistan was coordinated, to discuss the future of Afghanistan. Franks had already visited the big players in Pakistan and had held meetings with the Northern Alliance. He explained that the plan was not to take over Afghanistan, and he encouraged Dobbins to establish an interim government of the Afghan opposition as soon as possible so the US military could concentrate on al-Qaeda. Halfway through their meeting, an aide entered the room, telling Franks, "We have Karzai—our helicopter has just crossed the border." Franks explained to Dobbins: "Karzai is a Pashtun leading a small group of insurgents in the south. He was in danger and so he asked us to help him and we did. He's now on his way to Pakistan. We don't want any more Abdul Haq incidents, you understand."

In the following days Dobbins saw Karzai's name repeatedly in the chaos of notes, plans, and scenarios, and Dobbins concluded that Karzai had good connections on all sides of the Afghan political scene. Although neighbouring Pakistan still supported the Taliban and the Northern Alliance would rather have their own man in the presidential palace, Dobbins said they were in fact negotiating a compromise for a potential candidate in the first weeks of November. Turkey, a solid Northern Alliance ally, mentioned Karzai to Dobbins, based on preliminary talks they had had with Pakistan and the Northern Alliance in the previous weeks.

After the tip from Ankara, Dobbins flew to Pakistan and spoke with the Pakistani general Ehsan ul-Haq of the secret service (ISI). He also mentioned Karzai as a possible new leader, Dobbins says. Karzai wasn't Pakistan's first choice, but Dobbins sensed that General Haq realised his country couldn't make too many demands now that "their" Taliban regime was gradually collapsing.

A few days later, Karzai's name came up again when Dobbins met with Dr. Abdullah Abdullah, a Northern Alliance representative. He belonged to the Alliance's younger generation and he was their contact for the Americans. He spoke perfect English, was always dressed in Western clothing but had problems representing the strongly divided Alliance. He had compiled a list of about twenty names of potential leaders for a future Afghanistan.[90] Abdul Haq was on the list, as were the former minister of finance Amin Arsala, who served under the king in the seventies; the former army commander Rahim Wardak, who had been involved in the fight against the Soviets; several representatives of the old elite who hadn't lived in Afghanistan for years; and Karzai. Abdullah didn't find Karzai to be very prominent or well-known in Afghanistan, but his father was influential, and Hamid Karzai had always lived close to Afghanistan and never left for the U.S. Abdullah Abdullah saw that Karzai was committed to his country during the Taliban regime, which was a benefit. The Northern Alliance was already well acquainted with him even before 9/11. Karzai had sought contact with the Northern Alliance leader, Ahmed Shah Massoud.

It surprised Dobbins that part of the Northern Alliance and their nemesis, Pakistan, seemed to agree on a presidential candidate, Dobbins: "I don't think they had spoken of this with each other, because if they had been aware of it, they wouldn't have agreed to Karzai. We told each party that it was an interesting proposition, that's all." Dobbins believed this was prudent because it was far from certain that all the leaders of the Northern Alliance would accept Karzai as president. Rabbani, still officially the president, would have none of it and was already on his way to Kabul to take up his old position in the palace. Dobbins didn't deem it necessary to contact Karzai at the military base in Jacobabad, where he and his men from Uruzgan were hiding. Dobbins: "I don't think he was there to be interviewed about the presidency. He was almost captured by the Taliban and had to be taken to safety—that's all. Looking back you can say it turned out that way, but I think that at the time no one was sure Hamid Karzai would become the president."

Karzai also denied he was preparing his presidency in Jacobabad. "Everything happened without me," he said. Although Karzai now insists he never left Jacobabad, two diplomats later reported seeing him at the U.S. Embassy residence in Islamabad. Karzai attended a busy reception where he met the American ambassador Wendy Chamberlin, who at the time didn't realise she was meeting Afghanistan's future president.[91] She spoke with him only briefly before being distracted by a call from Washington, but not before Karzai pointed out to Chamberlin—who was predominantly focused on massaging Pakistan and the Northern Alliance—that the Pashtun must not be forgotten in the conflict.

In the meantime, at the American base in Jacobabad, preparations were underway for Karzai's return to Afghanistan, this time together with the CIA and Amerine's A-team. Food and clothing for the people in Uruzgan were parachuted in bundles. The packages contained powdered MRE's—Meals Ready to Eat – and wasn't universally appreciated in Uruzgan. Some anti-American residents of Tarin Kot burned them, while others sold them at the bazaar. The Americans also dropped fliers over Uruzgan depicting bin Laden with the Taliban leader Mullah Omar on a leash, like a dog.

NINE

The Fall of Tarin Kot

A MERINE'S A-TEAM PLANNED to accompany Karzai to Afghanistan to finish the job. The mission in Uruzgan would now be reinforced by the Americans. The commandos were in a hurry: in other parts of the country the A-teams and their Afghan allies had already taken a lot of territory from the Taliban and Kabul could fall any day now. At first Amerine didn't even understand him when Karzai mentioned their destination, "Tarin what?" he asked. He had never heard of it, but the map resolved the problem. "Ah, Tarin Koowt," Amerine repeated. Karzai explained that it was still too early for Kandahar City. The Taliban were armed to the teeth there, and unlike Tarin Kot, Kandahar is located on a plain, making it much more difficult to attack.

The Americans listened closely to Karzai but they were also concerned about his support in the region. The commandos needed to be sure there would be a strong base of insurgents to start the ball rolling. With only 12 Americans, they were concerned about the potential for large attacks of dozens of Taliban. There was also no other team active in the south. Amerine was honoured that he had been asked to "do" the south, but some preparation would have been nice. In the north, powerful warlords always have a private army at their disposal. Uzbek general Dostum, for instance, could have mustered three hundred men in no time. Amerine would have liked Karzai to deliver a few hundred fighters as well, but it wasn't clear that Karzai could deliver such numbers – or that he would even be welcomed with open arms.

With no time to spare, the helicopters were ordered. Graig, the CIA agent, explained the plan to the Afghans. The men were told they had to go in advance to Uruzgan and set up a base in Durji as soon as possible. Karzai and the twelve American Special Forces soldiers, along with a CIA team, would join them later.

The Afghans immediately started complaining. Were they being sent ahead as cannon fodder? Not everyone sitting on the bunker's cold concrete floor felt like re-entering the fight. But there really wasn't much choice. The Americans gave them GPS equipment and they were flown back to Afghanistan.

A dust cloud surrounded the helicopters when they landed in Durji. With the risk of attacks, the pilots wanted to touch down as briefly as possible, and the Afghans had to disembark quickly. The men held on tightly to their turbans and their billowing *shalwar kameeses* as they sprinted away from the helicopter's powerful rotor wash.

There was more disappointment to follow. They spent the night clambering up the mountains to get to the home of Mohammed Lal, who was with them and whose house they had used a few weeks earlier for the weapons drop. Lal had good relations with the Taliban, and it was safe, he had assured them. Although several of his relatives worked for the Taliban, they chose to keep their mouths shut about Karzai and his plans. Now, a little over a week later, the situation was completely different. Nobody was left in Durji – Lal's kala was deserted. While they had been safe in Jacobabad, many of those who remained, including the family of Lal, were punished and detained. Lal didn't think for very long: he quit 'Karzai's uprising' on the spot, and asked the others to leave immediately. At a loss, they walked off into the mountains.[92]

One of the remaining five grabbed a satellite telephone to update Karzai on the situation. "You can't come here," the man yelled into the telephone. "You'll have to think of something else." Desperate, the men walked on to the town of Deh Rawud, where they eventually found lodging. Once there, Karzai's three security guards from Kandahar—the Haji Mund, Haji Hafizullah, and Mohammed Shah—threw in the towel. There was nothing more they could do here, and Karzai couldn't get anything done in Uruzgan. After long deliberations they decided to return to Quetta, Pakistan. The journey back was hard on the men; there were many Taliban along the route, and numerous other groups trying to assert control over their own areas. Chaos reigned in the villages and along the road. The men took turns coming up with plausible excuses that would get them past active Taliban checkpoints. They stayed in Kandahar city for one night and arrived in Quetta the next day.

Instead of going home, Karzai's most important security guard Mohammed Shah soon defected, joining the ranks of Karzai's strongest competitor Gul Agha Sherzai, "the Lion of Kandahar." Mohammed Shah knew Sherzai from the 1990s when he was governor of Kandahar province and they were fighting together against an emergent Taliban. They both fled to Quetta after suffering battlefield losses. At the time Sherzai often worked with Karzai, but now he had new support structures. He had always enjoyed good relations with the Pakistanis, who would like to see him as Kandahar's governor again. Pakistan saw "its" Taliban disappearing, but they considered Sherzai to be their last chance to hold on to the important trade town of Kandahar and to maintain their influence in vital southern Afghanistan. Shortly after September 11, Karzai had asked Sherzai to join him, but now it seemed the Lion of Kandahar had other plans, and the race was on to see who would get to Kandahar city first. With the support of the American troops and the CIA, he was gathering a militia in the refugee camps at the border near Quetta and preparing his own invasion.

The loss of the base in Durji meant a change of plans. This time Karzai turned to his fellow tribesmen in Deh Rawud, men who had proven their loyalty by helping Karzai in Durji: the brothers Haji Bahadur and Haji Zahir Agha, Ibrahim as well as his brother Gilani – the Afghan who delivered the letter on behalf of Mullah Baradar to Karzai. They were all Popolzai, closely connected to each other and to Karzai. From Pakistan Karzai called Haji Bahadur, also known as "the Hero," to tell him he would be arriving soon. The Hero had disappeared rather quickly during the first attack in Durji, and hadn't returned after the failed weapons drop. It was a controversial move. Among Karzai's followers the Hero was perceived as a deserter who ran at the very first sign of the Taliban. But Karzai needed all the support he could find, and the fact that the Hero was Popolzai would help bind him to Karzai.

Around 7 a.m. on November 14, high in the mountains near Deh Rawud, the Hero assembled four large stacks of wood and set them alight, creating an improvised landing zone. In the early morning he watched the sky expectantly, together with a group of cousins and other Popolzai.

Three helicopters came quickly.[93] The men of ODA 574 and the CIA agents had initially planned to parachute in, but the weather was too severe, so the pilots landed their aircraft briefly on the vast plain while the group jumped out. The Americans were fully aware that Karzai didn't have enough fighters, but they had to act now. Everything seemed to be shifting in Afghanistan. Kabul had fallen, and Tarin Kot and Kandahar could be next. Anything could happen—there was even some concern that the Northern Alliance would attempt to take the latter. The team was ready to go, heavily armed and equipped with several laptops, radios, and thousands of dollars. When the helicopters left and the dust settled, they realised where they had just landed. They looked around, their jaws dropping as they found themselves on a vast mountain plateau. "This is the dark side of the moon," Amerine yelled across the mountain landscape. The tall Western men, some of them sporting nearly full beards, in modern bomber jackets, zip-off pants, and baseball caps stomped through the sand in this medieval scene where some houses are still built in caves.

The Hero enjoyed the spectacle, Americans walking with Karzai toward him.[94] He took their bags and loaded them on pack mules. He showed them how to walk downhill. "You must put your hands on one another's shoulders and descend in a line," he instructed them sternly. It was obvious to him that they were still not yet accustomed to the mountainous terrain. Later he bought them Afghan clothes, eighteen *shalwar kameeses* and eighteen turbans. That night the soldiers and the Afghans bedded down on thin mats in the *kota* of the Hero's brother, Haji Zahir Agha. The Americans slept in a long row along one wall of the square *kota*. A few commandos kept watch.

The following day, when they slowly got moving toward Tarin Kot in a ragtag convoy of ten cars, it looked like Tarin Kot was already about to fall. "Quite a lot of men in the town have already risen up against the Taliban," Karzai told Amerine. The American commando reacted flabbergasted. This is much too soon, he thought, looking back in consternation at the group of men trying to follow him. They weren't strong enough to support a revolt in Tarin Kot, and it would take at least another day before they got there. Amerine tried to calm Karzai down, and explained that the uprising had to wait until they had built themselves up into a capable fighting force. Karzai understood. "Can you stop them?" Amerine asked. "I'll do my best," says Karzai, while he dialled another phone number.

Amerine was still worried. Additional assurances were essential before driving into a town in chaos. He ordered the first car in the convoy to stop. Only a few words were needed to explain his men the situation in Tarin Kot. The communications sergeant opened up the antennae of his radio transmitter and contacted the American Regional Headquarters in Uzbekistan for as many weapons and ammunition as possible. A few hours later the first helicopters arrived. Pallets of supplies were lowered to the teams on the ground. There was almost too much for the modest convoy, and Amerine had his men strap the weapons to the roofs of their vehicles. He got into the first car again, and instructed the driver to make haste, while commandos laid on top of the stacks of weapons to keep them from falling off.

While driving through the deserted plains of Deh Rawud, Karzai told the commandos the bad news. The Taliban had already been driven out of Tarin Kot. It had even been rumoured that the Taliban mayor had been hung from a pole in the city. As if this news wasn't disappointing enough, Karzai's sources also heard that 'fresh' Taliban-fighters were on their way from Kandahar city to attack Hamid Karzai and his American supporters. Frantically Karzai tried to mobilise more men, contacting everyone via his messengers and the satellite telephone. Some of his fighter were relieved and surprised to hear he was still alive. The last they had heard of him was that he hadn't survived the battle near Durji. But most of the 'insurgents' were hesitant to join Karzai again. Some feared the Taliban, others didn't believe in Karzai any more. "Look up at the sky," Karzai said to one of them. "You will see an American aircraft now and then. They are here to help us, but be sure to wave a white flag from your car window, so the pilots realise you are innocent." Some were convinced and got back into their cars.

Karzai and the Americans tried to increase the convoy's tempo. A few Afghans on their donkeys had trouble keeping up with the cars. East of Deh Rawud, en route to Tarin Kot, they crossed into open plains, where they were completely exposed. There was no way to avoid it so they kept driving. It was a strange procession, and when Amerine looked back at the convoy, he laughed out loud at the sight of it: Twenty pick-up trucks, some horses, donkeys, vans, and a few old U.N. jeeps. His Afghan driver tried to avoid the worst bumps. Karzai was seated between him and the driver, and he continued making calls in Pashto.

Amerine took out his notebook and tried to write down what he heard, even though he didn't know how to spell it. He needed to be careful not to record information that would reveal their strategy to the Taliban if captured. He caught a glimpse of Deh Rawud. He knew many Taliban were born in Uruzgan and that even the Taliban leader, Mullah Omar, had lived north of the town. It was strange to be driving through what was the enemy's heartland. He wondered where Omar might be at this very moment. Out of the corner of his eye he could also see remains of the war against the Soviets, a dramatic panorama of past foreign invasions that scrolled by like a reel of film. A bullet-riddled well with a U.N. logo, carcasses of Soviet tanks like old fossils in the landscape. The Afghans used materials from them to reinforce the walls of their *kalas*. At least this way it still served a purpose, Amerine thought.

The convoy finally rode into Tarin Kot with the American commandos in the front, Karzai and the CIA operatives behind them, followed by dozens of Afghans. The event went unnoticed by the international media. All attention was focused on Kabul, which had fallen to the Northern Alliance just a few days earlier. Meanwhile, large numbers of al-Qaeda operatives were escaping from Kandahar and the northern cities into Pakistan. There had been no effective blockade set up against these "refugees." In the south the Taliban still stubbornly defended their positions. As he rode into Tarin Kot, Amerine wondered anxiously how it would all end.

At first sight the situation didn't seem all that bad. No dead bodies in the ditches like in Kabul—barely any signs of heavy combat. Hidden behind the mud brick walls of the small houses on the main road, the Uruzganis stared intently at Amerine. He waved, but the shadows retreated into the *kalas*. Amerine sent his men into the centre of town to scout it out.

*   *   *

SAID HAD LED a wandering existence in the Tarin Kot suburbs while Karzai was safely in Pakistan. After having been detained by the Taliban during the raid and subsequently bluffing his way to freedom, he had been in hiding at six different addresses. He saw the two helicopters as they flew away from Durji in the direction of Pakistan, but he had no way of knowing that Karzai had been in one of them. Every day he listened to the BBC World Service to stay abreast of the latest news. While it was all he could do to stay out of Taliban hands, he heard that elsewhere the Taliban had given up five or six provinces already. Good news. The newscaster reported they had given up a village near Kandahar, which was even more reassuring. Were his own people finally joining the revolt? Said travelled on to Deh Rawud, where he could feel safer. As he approached the town he came across a crowd of people on their way to Tarin Kot, jubilantly shouting that the Taliban were history. Said had no idea what was going on there, and hadn't been back since Karzai flew into the mountains, but he decided to join them. He passed Talani, Jan Mohammed's hometown. There too, people were celebrating the departure of the local Taliban. Said met some enthusiastic relatives who were surprised to see him. "Where were you, where have you been?" they asked him. "Do you even realise what's going on? The Taliban have fled!"

Meanwhile in Tarin Kot, news of the Taliban governor's departure was making the rounds. Karzai supporters who had already spoken with him before Karzai's arrival in Tarin Kowt, didn't use a weapon but made him clear that his time was over. After this talk, he left everything behind and went to the Mirabad Valley, just east of Tarin Kot. The first looting had started, though. The townspeople of Tarin Kot went to the bazaar's market booths in search of money, weapons and merchandise. Said observed from a distance and worried about the chaos in town. He went to the city hall, which by now was empty. The mayor had left, and, contrary to rumours, he wasn't hanging from a pole or murdered in any other fashion. 'Rival' Mullah Shafiq, had offered him a safe place in his area. Feeling he had no choice, Said appointed himself mayor of Tarin Kot. No one else was stepping up to the task, and Said felt he had a right to the position since he had done so much for Karzai. He immediately issued his first order: Stop the looting. Whether his measures had any effect isn't clear.

Then a different mayor arrived, a Popolzai with more experience than Said. Khairo Jan had been in charge of Tarin Kot during the Taliban regime. The Taliban gave him the position in 1994 to appease tribes that had been shoved aside. Khairo Jan hadn't lasted long. Once the Taliban had secured their dominance in Uruzgan they got rid of him. He had invited a foreign journalist to come and visit the local bazaar and this was used as an excuse to fire him after less than six months.

Now that the Taliban were leaving, Khairo Jan decided to return. He had wanted to join Karzai earlier, but at that point Karzai had just been airlifted to Pakistan. Now he went to the city's prison with a group of Popolzai and Barakzai to release the inmates. They then went to the bazaar, where they told everyone the Taliban had left. The men proudly walked through the streets and invited the citizens of Tarin Kot to join them. They felt they were back in business in Uruzgan, although many residents were still waiting to see how the situation would pan out. Amid all the anarchy everyone was cautious, but the end of the

Taliban seemed by now to be inevitable. "Northern Afghanistan had largely fallen by then," Khairo Jan later recalled. "The Taliban realized this, so they fled to the mountains. They didn't even put up a fight—it was over in no time."

Many Karzai supporters wondered where the man who had set all this in motion was. Some were afraid for their safety. What would come next now the city had fallen? They were in charge, but what should they do? They asked Said to go find Karzai, but the self-appointed mayor had no idea where to look. Others took over the job, going through the neighbourhoods of Tarin Kot where various elders had taken over from the Taliban. In one neighbourhood it was the Barakzai, in another the Popolzai. So shortly after the Taliban's departure, Tarin Kot already seemed to have split up into tribal territories. And still Karzai was nowhere to be found. Other messengers were sent to areas outside Tarin Kot, to Char Chino, Deh Rawud, and even to Quetta, where Karzai's half-brother Ahmad Wali still resided. News arrived from Quetta that Karzai's half-brother knew exactly where he was and that Karzai could arrive in Tarin Kot any minute now.

While the Popolzai were getting ready to take over Tarin Kot and the province, in the capital the Barakzai leader Rozi Khan also arrived. He hadn't supported Karzai because he had a long-standing feud with Jan Mohammed, Karzai's ally. Many men on both sides had died, and even Karzai himself had barely escaped with his life. Now Rozi Khan was eager to enjoy some of the spoils. For six years he had held on to a large weapons cache somewhere in northern Uruzgan, through bribes, excuses, and thanks to connections within the Taliban. Armed with these weapons he entered the city. Rozi Khan went to the governor's compound first, but it was empty. Next he went to the police station where a battle ensued with the Taliban, who tried not to give up what was effectively their last stock of weapons. But the Taliban lost. Five of them were killed along with four of Rozi Khan's men. After the Taliban fled, Khan's men entered the police station and seized the weapons they found inside.

*   *   *

KARZAI WAS NERVOUS when he drove into the centre of Tarin Kot. He wondered what the Uruzganis would think of his American allies. Of course, there would still be conservative Muslims who wanted nothing to do with these Western heathens. Then there were those who were disappointed in the Americans because they disappeared after the war against the Soviets. So the city could very well be uncomfortable with his group. But when he arrived he was immediately taken to the governor's deserted white mansion as if he was the region's new leader. There, several old fighters rejoined him: Mualim Rahmatullah, Abdul Ghani Mama, Sultan Mohammed, and even Rozi Khan.

Karzai was relieved. Immediately he gestured to Amerine to be seated. "They are incredibly happy with us and with you," Amerine heard Karzai saying. He explained how Uruzgan works: "They have high expectations now. You can rely on these people. The real Taliban warriors are no longer here. They are in Kandahar, where they have their headquarters. That's where they will put up the biggest fight. Here they are merely farmers, landowners, and small businessmen. They are all poor, dreadfully poor. For them the question is always: who must I support in order to survive? Whether it's the Taliban or someone else is immaterial. At this moment their hopes are fixed on us." Amerine shifted his legs in an effort to stay sitting cross-legged on the cold floor of Karzai's new place. The room was lined with Persian rugs and they were served steaming cups of tea and large dishes of food. It was almost peaceful as the gas light flickered on the Uruzganis' faces. They all looked towards Karzai. As far as Amerine was concerned, the first *shura* (meeting) about the future of Tarin Kot could now begin.

Karzai's telephone once again disturbed the peace. In the few days Amerine had been on the road with Karzai, he had learned how essential the telephone was to him. It was his principal weapon. He used it to stay in touch with his informants. They saw everything coming, and they warned him about everything. Although Karzai didn't always translate everything for Amerine, this time he did. "Three to five hundred Taliban forces are heading this way," he told the American. "They want me, dead or alive." Karzai said it calmly, without a trace of nerves or panic. He even made a giggling joke: "Maybe they'll come on foot." Amerine grinned—anything was possible in Afghanistan. The mood quickly turned serious again. The first Taliban forces would be arriving in Tarin Kot within a few hours.

Karzai seemed unruffled, though, and he continued to

eat. He gestured to Amerine to do the same. Amerine was bewildered. "It's important to defend the city and my life," Karzai said, "but this doesn't mean we shouldn't celebrate the first day of Ramadan." Ramadan will be a problem, Amerine realised. His operation would coincide with the four weeks of Muslim fasting. Karzai's men would be much weaker than usual because they wouldn't be eating during the day. He wondered if the Taliban would do the same.

Reluctantly, Amerine picked at the mutton on the platters and tore off a piece of *naan* bread. He had to restrain himself from getting up and getting on with it. He wondered if Karzai realised what was going to happen. After 10 minutes, he couldn't wait any longer. "There's something I have to do," he told Karzai, apologising profusely and taking his leave of the group. As he left the *kota* he said: "When they're done, please ask these elders to send their men to the town centre—I will need all of them." Karzai nodded. Amerine crossed the narrow street in a few bounds, to where his eleven commandos were waiting in their recently established makeshift headquarters. Amerine briefed them, allowing no discussion. He nodded to his communications sergeant, Yoshita, who transmitted to their headquarters in Uruzgan the message that the Taliban would be arriving within hours.

* * *

SAID WAS THE first to encounter the angry Taliban troops moving toward Tarin Kot from Kandahar. He sat with around fourteen men in a small building on the road southeast from Tarin Kot. When they had heard the same rumour that the Taliban were coming, they had stolen cars from the Department of Education and escaped. Said hadn't realised until now how big the Taliban group would be. Late in the evening after their Ramadan meal, they prayed in the valley behind their *kota* and took up strategic positions. They were ready, and even during their prayers they looked up every now and then. They heard the Taliban convoy in the distance, announcing their approach with a loud *Allah-u Akhbar* that echoed in the mountains. The sound was so loud that Said knew they wouldn't defeat the Taliban. He didn't hesitate. He took his slippers in hand and started running for the mountains.

It didn't take long before the first American fighter jets flew over Tarin Kot. Transmitting updates to Amerine and his A-team, everybody could see the Taliban convoy left Kandahar city and was heading for Tarin Kot at full speed. Amerine now realised this was serious. "Let's smoke 'em," he screamed, shocked at his own words. Usually this even-keeled man in his thirties doesn't use such coarse language—but this wasn't a normal situation, he justified to himself.

Amerine went back to Karzai and asked him where his men were. The Americans were only twelve, and he wanted to have a large group of Uruzganis with him to conquer the Taliban. But when he gathered Karzai's men outside the compound, only about thirty showed up, which was not nearly enough. It was obvious to the Americans: Karzai didn't have enough leverage with his tribesmen to form a militia. But there was no time to wait. Karzai's fighters were loaded into the borrowed cars and together with the Americans, they left Tarin Kot around 4 a.m. Karzai stayed in the city.

They drove straight to a high plateau outside of town. Amerine needed to be able to see the enemy in order to accurately assess the level of threat. It was anyone's guess which route the Taliban would take. They could come straight across the valley, on-road, off-road, or across a mountain pass. "Enjoy the scenery while you can," Amerine said cynically. One of his men peered at the road through his binoculars. He only saw a small car parked on the shoulder. He lowered the binoculars and handed them to his commander. Soon an enormous dust cloud indicated that things were about to get even more serious. Dozens of cars raced in a line towards the valley; regular jeeps, SUVs, and other vehicles with anti-tank rockets were swiftly approaching Tarin Kot.

Yoshita, the communications sergeant, grabbed a small device that had become typical of the war in Afghanistan. It was a target designator, a laser device with which commandos on the ground could designate for bomber jets in the air the exact locations for precision airstrikes. At that moment there were indeed "barely any boots on the ground," as the American Secretary of Defense put it, but there were plenty of planes in the air. The Uruzgani insurgents stood around the small group of Americans and had no idea what was about to happen. When should they start fighting? Yoshita aimed his laser device at the first cars in the convoy. The target's exact coordinates were signalled to the fighter jet pilots and the bombs began to fall. The first one missed its target. It was 5 a.m. and the sun was rising. Around him Amerine saw the Afghans' disappointment. The next bomb, however, was a bull's eye, and so was the one after that. Suddenly the air was full of American fighter jets dropping one bomb after another on the convoy.

To Amerine's surprise the airstrike did not impress the Afghans. They stood awkwardly behind the Americans, looking down at their shoes. They were no longer doing anything and they wanted to leave as quickly as possible. They had never seen this kind of warfare. Countless Taliban forces were moving toward them and they were no more than forty men. They thought this would not end well. Amerine saw himself surrounded by suspicious brown eyes. They didn't see any troops, no armed men entering the battle. They had no idea how effective the Americans could be with these air attacks.

"We won't win this," the oldest Afghan said to Amerine, gesturing to the valley in front of him. Before Amerine could even respond, the Afghans took off. It didn't matter how many assurances Amerine yelled at them in English, they had no effect, perhaps thanks to the language barrier. The American was unnerved. While the bombs continued to drop further ahead, his defence was suddenly gone. The cars were started – all of them. Amerine had briefly forgotten the advice he was once given during training: always keep your car keys with you. He realised he had to leave now too, and quickly—staying behind with only his American commandos wasn't an option. He jumped into the back of one of the pick-up trucks and saw his commandos do the same. The Afghans drove full throttle back to Tarin Kot.

And so in a short time there was nothing left of Amerine's defense. The rain of bombs ceased immediately when the jets stopped receiving precise coordinates. The Taliban were headed for Tarin Kot. The Americans had learned via radio that the Taliban cars were mainly ferrying Pakistanis and Arabs, men who had nothing to lose, Amerine concluded. While the Afghan Taliban could surrender and eventually return to their villages, it was a whole different ball game for the foreign fighters. They would fight to death under any circumstances. If something wasn't done soon, Tarin Kot would be embroiled in a bloody battle.

Back in the provincial capital everything was quiet. No one seemed to be aware of the events happening in Kandahar. When the Americans arrived in Karzai's compound and reported their early withdrawal, the Afghan leader was furious with the failure of yet another plan. "This isn't what we agreed!" he yelled at the Afghans. Their nerves – those of both Karzai and his men – were frayed. After Karzai's fire-and-brimstone speech, the Afghans had no choice. Together with Amerine, they raced back along the same trail. But they didn't get far. Amerine pulled up near a cemetery outside the city and realized immediately that the enemy had drawn much closer. By now the Taliban were three miles from Tarin Kot. Amerine and his A-team quickly re-established contact with the pilots and tried to transform the armed Uruzganis into a rear guard.

Everything the U.S. Air Force had available in Afghanistan was redirected to Tarin Kot. One bomb after another exploded in the valley. Heavy smoke clouds appeared everywhere. The airstrikes lasted for hours—they seemed inescapable. Yoshita pointed out all the jeeps relatively easily with his laser device, and they were destroyed, one by one. Hundreds of Taliban were killed, and by midday they had lost the battle.

The final moments of the battle were intense. Four Toyotas carrying a total of ten Taliban had managed to escape the bombing. They pushed on to the city's defence line. Large groups of citizens emerged from their *kalas* to protect Tarin Kot and their families. Fighter jets couldn't do much here. The Taliban were too close to the busy bazaar. In this final battle on the gates of Tarin Kot, twelve civilians were killed.

Heavy combat also took place that day around Mirabad, a few miles northeast of Tarin Kot, where many Taliban had fled after the fall of the city. Karzai called Rozi Khan for assistance, and he was able to defeat the Taliban near the village of Naji Chin. One of his men was killed.

When Amerine thought the battle of Tarin Kot had finally been won, he suddenly heard loud gunfire in the centre of town. He wondered what was going on. Perhaps some other Taliban forces that he overlooked? It turned out to be celebratory gunfire. Amerine walked over to Karzai and laughed, relieved: "The ammunition could be put to better use, so could you please stop them?" Soon everything was quiet again. A few men were detained as punishment.

Inside their mud brick headquarters, the eleven commandos were slumped against the wall, the sleeping bags they had brought piled in a corner. The Afghans had given them some extra blankets to guard against the cold floor – not that they had gotten round to sleeping yet. Two long antennae stuck out above their compound and laptops created a surreal blue glow. Newly delivered weapons and supplies were in the yard of the compound, guarded by Afghans. Helicopters continued to provide with weapons and food. One of Americans walked by the Afghans on watch and had to prod one awake. But the A-team couldn't care less. They were keyed up on the moment, the sort of difficult battle they had prepared long and hard for in America.

Amerine joined Karzai and his elders. Finally a moment of peace. The commandos hadn't been in the region three days and already had experienced their first attack. Tarin Kot was still in their hands and Karzai still alive. Only hours after the battle, Karzai was surrounded by a bigger group of elders who now knew they would continue to support Karzai and not the Taliban. Amerine observed them sitting around Karzai. A small dark man had also joined the group and he didn't look too friendly. He was seated across from Amerine and he glared at him long and suspiciously. The American felt pretty uncomfortable. When he had had enough, he asked Karzai who the man was. "He's a Taliban combatant—he has taken a loss," said Karzai. Amerine immediately reached for the pistol stuck in the back of his pants and with his other hand he gives the man an amicable slap on the shoulder. Although they didn't understand each other, they laughed loudly, and the ice was broken.

"It was fantastic, unbelievable!", the tribal elders told

Karzai again and again. The enthusiasm of the elders around Karzai for the deeds of the Americans on this first day of Ramadan was rising by the minute. All their previous hesitation – the fear, the insecurity – all vanished after this spectacular action. Now they had an ally with whom they could defeat the Taliban, an ally with weapons, fighter jets, equipment they didn't even know existed. They had fought with American weapons themselves in the eighties, against the Soviets, but this was something else. Although in the beginning they were skeptical of only fighting with airplanes, what really impressed them was the precision, the efficiency and the speed, of these helicopters and jets. The way the Americans simply crushed the Taliban was beyond them. The Americans seemed omnipotent, able to do anything, to find and hit any target no matter how deep the cave or remote the location. The Afghans cheered.

The Taliban surrendered en masse in the north when danger loomed, but they still hadn't given up in the south. This became apparent the next day. A message arrived saying that a new convoy was on its way to Tarin Kot, only this time it was a lot smaller. Karzai, already worried about the hazards to innocent civilians, proposed a moratorium on bombing convoys of three cars or less. "Let those be our own little Rules of Engagement," he told Amerine.[95] The American continued to authorise new airstrikes almost daily, and dozens more combatants died on the road from Kandahar to Tarin Kot.

Karzai kept on contacting his people with his phone. One moment a spokesman from the Taliban would be on the line to negotiate, another it would be someone from the Northern Alliance or Karzai's half-brother. In between he received various people in his *kala*. A local farmer asked for a donkey in return for supporting the uprising. Karzai enjoyed arranging these kinds of affairs. He would wink, act semi-important, or whisper his amazement to Amerine about a neighbour arguing with his cousin. "We will solve this," he said when the man was done. He translated the discussion for Amerine, who found it all quite entertaining. Now and again it was pure theatre. Afghans dropped by, shouting and waving their hands as they turned a molehill into a mountain, Karzai proved he could also be forceful. In a loud voice he ordered the men to end their quarrel and then sent them away.

While Amerine and his men recovered from the battle, Washington sent some unsettling news. The mission in Uruzgan would now be a top priority for the Bush administration, and Amerine was under-ranked for it—it could no longer be left up to a mere captain. A so-called "C-team" was to be flown in: three officers who would normally be in charge of three A-teams and who rarely go out into the field themselves. One of the three officers, a broad-shouldered Lieutenant Colonel by the name of David Fox, would coordinate Amerine's mission from this point forward. At the same time he would be in charge of a different A-team that had joined Karzai's rival – Gul Agha Sherzai—that was moving on Kandahar city from the southeast. Karzai was no longer the only resistance leader in the south.

TEN

The Unexpected Voice at the Bonn Conference

THE C-TEAM WAS amazed at the primitive circumstances they found on arrival at Amerine's *kala*.[96] One of them was Major Donald Bolduc, a mayor's son from Laconia, New Hampshire. So this is where we start, the short soldier with blond hair thought. He had been in the U.S. Army for years, like his two brothers, but this mission was different, even for the experienced soldier. The C-team really only had information about the war in northern Afghanistan, and very little was known about their destination in the south. In Quetta they had tried to get a clear picture of Taliban strength in Kandahar, with little success. The name Hamid Karzai hadn't meant anything to him either, until he was briefed by the CIA. The mission was unusual in that he and his men had had to infiltrate quickly into a hostile area, but with very little intelligence preparation – something he had never done before.

Before flying to Uruzgan, the C-team had to wait at a hermetically sealed Pakistani airbase west of Quetta. They had meant to leave earlier, but the weather had kept them grounded. Once they were in Afghan airspace, they quickly became aware of the Taliban. In the north they had fallen like dominoes, but in the south the resistance was still strong. Their helicopter was repeatedly fired at from the ground. Bolduc saw the rockets whiz by. The cannon on the ground lit up the night sky. They flew "tactically", zigzagging along steep mountain ridges, trying to avoid ground fire. To make matters worse, Bolduc's helicopter began to experience mechanical problems. He didn't know what was amiss, but he suspected an oil leak. For a long time they flew at half power over Taliban gunfire. They briefly debated turning back—they were at high risk of being shot down or crashing in hostile terrain. Their pilot decided to press on to Tarin Kot. Finally they made an emergency landing on a dusty, tamped down landing strip. The men disembarked, and Bolduc got out his GPS. He needed to leave the exposed location as soon as possible. On the west side a group of men were supposed to be ready to take them. At first nothing could be seen in the dark, cold night. Then small lights glimmered in the distance. In the pick-up trucks of local Afghans, who didn't say a word, they rode to Amerine's compound.

They didn't have much with them—a few pieces of clothing, some weapons and ammunition—so they could travel light and fast. They carried over US$250,000, the bills hidden in small parcels. The money was theirs to spend, a blank cheque, and no need for filling out receipts. With it they could bribe enemy troops.

"Oh my God," exclaimed Bolduc, as he walked Amerine's compound. No running water, no electricity, nothing. The windows were covered with flaps of plastic that did little to keep out the continuous dust clouds. Bolduc had just come from the Jordanian desert, where they had trained in secret. They had stayed in tents, and that was a luxury compared to where they were now.

When the C-team arrived, the mood in Karzai's *kala* was upbeat. Because of the success of the battle of Tarin Kot, local militants were still arriving. Bolduc looked in amazement at the many men who were suddenly no longer Taliban. He wasn't used to this. He had seen a lot of conflicts, but the speed with which people change sides here was something he had never experienced before. It worried him a little. Yesterday they were Taliban, today they supported Karzai. What will happen tomorrow, he wondered—who could he trust? All those village elders, farmers and ex-Taliban combatants gathered in his compound. Cultural and language barriers meant Bolduc had little control of the situation in the crowded courtyard. Dealing with this was not part of his training. The only thing he could do was take these men at their word.

One morning a group of approximately five hundred men stood in the broad street in front of Amerine's compound. "What, in God's name, are they doing here?" Bolduc cried out. "They belong with us now, sir," his interpreter said. Bolduc laughed and immediately took action. Every time defectors were sent to him, he addressed them. He stood in the dusty courtyard opposite the small kitchen where a cooking fire burned practically non-stop. Big pieces of *naan* bread and live chickens were carried inside to feed everyone. Against this background Bolduc explained to the group what the Americans were doing here. One man from Deh Rawud, who spoke some English, did his best to translate: "We are here to help one of yours. Hamid. He's a great soldier and political leader and together with him we plan to defeat the Taliban. And we really need your help to do this." The men looked at him with interest and Bolduc felt he was truly making a connection. He continued: "Right now we are going to feed you, okay? We will give you food first, next we will write down your names and you will get the equipment you need. And then you will test your weapons and we will integrate you into our military structure."[97]

The communication between the Afghans and the Americans was often hilarious. Names were too hard to remember, so the Americans quickly came up with nicknames. One of the Afghans was dubbed "Elvis," another the "sergeant-major," another "supply guy." The practice worked in reverse, too. Graig, the name of the secret agent, was the only one the Afghans could remember, though it was pronounced a number of ways— "Creek," "Graik. Graig already made his name with Karzai's men earlier on. When one of them once asked him to which tribe he would want to belong, he said he was a true Popolzai. The men – all Popolzai themselves – had cheered him loudly. And Graig asked the Afghans almost every day "*Tsenga yei?*" (How are you?) Even though he didn't understand the answers, it made everyone laugh.

* * *

MEANWHILE, FAR FROM Tarin Kot, in the capitals of the

countries involved in this war, diplomats were preparing to look to the future of Afghanistan. A few days ahead of the fall of Kabul, the decision was taken to hold a United Nations-led conference with the different Afghan opposition groups. Regional players Pakistan, Russia and Iran would be involved as well. Besides addressing the difficult Afghan problem, the countries lost time squabbling about the location of the conference.[98] Saudi Arabia and the United Arab Emirates were dropped because of their support for the Taliban. Berlin was suggested by UN-diplomats, but it was turned down because it would attract too much media. Königswinter, a smaller town near Bonn in western Germany, was eventually selected. The director of a luxury hotel on the Petersberg, frequently visited by royalty and national leaders, was asked to cancel all bookings in order to be ready for the big Afghanistan conference in November.[99] So the executive boards of T-Mobile and Siemens had to find another venue. A very different event was about to take place in the stately white mansion along the Rhine.

The international community wanted to end the chaos in Kabul as soon as possible. The Northern Alliance had already taken the city, and with no Americans or other international troops present, the city was already descending into chaos. Media mainly showed the victorious Alliance forces driving in jeeps and shouting loudly throughout the city. Meanwhile, looting was also going on and brutal murders were being committed, the victims were mainly Arabs and Pakistanis. It was an embarrassment for the international community. The war seemed adrift. The fear that the Northern Alliance would try to do it alone was underlined by the behaviour of its leader Rabbani. He had been president before the Taliban took control and in his opinion he was still officially the president. Because the Taliban was not recognised internationally, Rabbani was indeed still the leader, at least on paper. After the fall of the Taliban he immediately returned to the city to assume his position in the presidential palace. Many in Kabul weren't happy with Rabbani, a Tajik. Other ethnic groups like the Pashtuns and the Hazara feared a repeat of what happened after the departure of the Soviets and the fall of the communist regime. Then, as now, all kinds of militias entered Kabul and the city became tangled in a bloody civil war. The international community was concerned, too. The Americans had asked the Northern Alliance to agree not to take Kabul alone.[100] Yet when the time came, the desire for absolute power, and the perceived need to fill the power vacuum created by the departure of the Taliban was apparently too strong.

The conference in Germany had to lead to an interim government capable of taking over from the Northern Alliance as quickly as possible, until elections could be held. It would also have to ask for an international military force to keep the peace in Kabul. The crucial decision in the debate was who should lead the interim government.

* * *

LONG BEFORE 9/11 the United Nations had been working on a plan for an eventual post-Taliban Afghanistan.[101] After the al-Qaeda attack on the American warship *USS Cole* in 2000, the United Nations assumed that American intervention in Afghanistan was inevitable. This expectation was strengthened after the destruction of the UNESCO-protected Buddha statues in Bamyan province. Top U.N. officials feared that, in the case of a military intervention, the Americans would focus mainly on a partnership with the Northern Alliance, the only opposition group still holding territory within Afghanistan. However, the United Nations found the basis for the Northern Alliance too narrow, because the Pashtuns—the largest ethnic group in Afghanistan—were hardly represented. In order to defeat the largely Pashtun-supported Taliban, Pashtun leadership was essential for the opposition.

The United Nations concentrated on the so-called Rome Group, the supporters of the last Afghan king, Zahir Shah, who had been in the Italian capital after being deposed in 1973. The old Pashtun elite, most of whom hadn't lived in Afghanistan for years, had a strong preference for the return of the king, hoping that this would allow them to return to key positions in Afghanistan themselves. After it became apparent that the king would be unacceptable to the Northern Alliance, the question of who would be a suitable candidate remained unanswered.

The Americans had little faith in the exiles around the king, especially since the Northern Alliance vetoed his return.[102] The Americans had placed their bets on Karzai after several rounds of diplomatic consultation. The largest group, the Northern Alliance had already frequently spoken with Karzai about the fight against the Taliban. And, it already turned out, Karzai wasn't a big problem for Pakistan or Iran.

Thus, at the eve of the conference, the international community already considered Karzai one of the main leadership candidates for the interim government. The British ambassador in Kabul had whispered his name to a BBC reporter. And the Americans had convinced the Special Envoy of the United Nations, Lakhdar Brahimi, that Karzai was probably the best candidate. The American Special Envoy for the Afghan Opposition, James Dobbins, had also concluded that there were hardly any alternatives to Karzai; he was really the only candidate acceptable to the neighbouring countries of Pakistan, Russia, and Iran.

Certain elements within the Afghan opposition resisted the idea of a Pashtun president and required guarantees for the Uzbek, Tajik and Hazara groups. That's why more than a week before the conference, the United Nations promised the Northern Alliance several key ministerial positions in the future interim government.[103] The Alliance leader, the famed Ahmed Shah Massoud, had been killed shortly before September 11. His successor, General Fahim would become minister of defence. Internal affairs was reserved for Yunus Qanuni, and the Western-oriented Dr. Abdullah Abdullah was to be minister of foreign affairs. Both Qanuni and Abdullah were important figures in the Northern Alliance.

The diplomatic preliminaries pertaining to the Rome Group, on the other hand, did not go as smoothly. Although an important role for king Zahir Shah in the future Afghanistan had been set aside, there were other candidates for presidency within the Rome Group, such as the Uzbek Sattar Sirat, once the youngest minister under the king and now one of his most trusted fellow exiles. Amin Arsala, the king's minister of finance, also sought a senior position in post-Taliban Afghanistan. They had hardly been consulted since September 11, and no deal had been made with this group. Both leaders felt insulted by the United Nations and America, but refused to give up their political ambitions to defeat Karzai.[104]

Karzai didn't attend the Bonn conference. He claimed later that he was willing to go, but he couldn't travel at the time.[105] Some diplomats immediately questioned his absence. "Karzai, of all people, should be here," noted one European representative. "He is the diplomat and he has attended so many of these conferences already. Where is he?"[106] But the future leader was in Uruzgan, with no plans of leaving. His absence wasn't really a problem, though, since by now he had plenty of supporters who would defend his candidacy. The evening before the conference began, he received a call from one of the participants. "Rumour has it," the caller told Karzai, "that they are considering you."[107]

Nevertheless, there was some way to go yet. Even before the conference at Petersburg had fully begun, the Rome Group was ready with its objections. U.N. envoy Brahimi met with Sattar Sirat, the delegation's head. Like the Algerian Brahimi, Sirat spoke Arabic and Sirat complained that the Northern Alliance had a bigger delegation at the conference than did his Rome Group.

Brahimi conceded the point, but stood his ground when Sirat criticised him for giving away three of the most important ministerial positions to the Northern Alliance. "This doesn't leave much influence for the president," said Sirat. But Brahimi explained that this was the decision and that it couldn't be changed. Sirat accepted this and promised Brahimi that he would cooperate constructively in choosing an interim leader.

"It will have to be a Pashtun, though," Sirat recalled hearing Brahimi saying. Sirat was flabbergasted. He was an Uzbek and it was now obvious that he had no chance of becoming president. "How dare you say that and who is going to appoint this Pashtun?" Sirat asked. Brahimi mentioned Karzai by saying: "What do you think? After all, he's a friend of yours, isn't he?" Sirat claimed that Karzai was no friend and that the Rome Group wouldn't nominate him. He felt that Karzai didn't even really belong with the Rome Group. His father was the real leader in Sirat's eyes. They had been friends, and Sirat remembered he had always had a lot of Popolzai followers in the south. But his son? No, Sirat never had much of a rapport with him. The man always did whatever he wanted. "What are we even doing here?" he asked Brahimi. "It seems we have nothing to choose."

During the conference a decision would have to be made about new leadership, but also on a multinational military force, and a new constitution would need to be drafted. They had six days to do it all.

Four delegations gathered in the hotel's large classy *Jugendstil* conference room: the Rome Group, the Northern Alliance, the Peshawar Group, which was more or less aligned with Pakistan, and the smaller Cyprus Group, which had good connections with Iran.[108] The men and a few women greeted one another cordially. They shook hands, hugged one another, and took their seats at the large square table. The Taliban hadn't been invited—the Northern Alliance, which didn't want any more Pashtuns at the table, had successfully blocked them.

The German minister of foreign affairs, Joschka Fischer, opened the conference. He addressed the delegates with the Rhine in the background, where large cruise ships full of partying tourists floated by. Fischer argued that an historic compromise had to be made that week and that he was optimistic about the outcome.

U.N. envoy Lakhdar Brahimi was next to speak. He had decided to keep the international press at a distance during the conference, fearing that they would delay the negotiation process. He would also have liked to see as few non-Afghans in the room as possible. The Americans protested this because they felt Afghanistan was their war. Brahimi, too, gave an inspiring speech about the need for a breakthrough – they must reach an agreement here in Germany.

The Afghan delegations were next, and they also gave positive speeches. Each person spoke at length about his own ideas, about the hope that all would now be well with the country, that all had to do their best, and that there couldn't be too much foreign meddling, although international troops would have to be considered, at least for Kabul.

When all four delegations were done, something strange happened. Brahimi tapped the conference chairman on the shoulder and asked if he could add a few words. The chairman nodded. He was with the Northern Alliance and knew what was about to happen.[109] The old Algerian UN-diplomat with his wrinkled face bent toward the micro-phone: "Someone else would like to talk with us, from Afghanistan," he said. This took many of the participants by surprise. They wondered about who it could be. Only four groups had been invited. Brahimi nodded to the sound technician in the corner. A speaker was suspended from the ceiling by a long black wire, several feet above the table. Some had already been wondering what it was for. Suddenly Karzai's voice came through, live from Uruzgan.

This was such a bombshell that very few people in the classy room actually heard precisely what Karzai said in his six-minute speech. The specifics weren't important, though: Some generalisations about the situation in Afghanistan, how it was imperative that this conference succeed, and that everyone would be included once again in the *loya jirga*. What mattered was that Karzai had reached out via his satellite telephone, had established his presence even though he wasn't physically part of any of the delegations.[110]

When Karzai had finished talking a ruckus broke out in the room. The men of the Rome Group were especially shocked. The tall former army leader Amin Wardak of the Rome Group wanted to walk out, but was stopped by Amin Arsala, who yanked him back into his chair. When Wardak worked together with Karzai for a while during the

Taliban regime, trying to get American support, the two were often at odds. This voice from Uruzgan was too much for him. Amin Arsala was also unpleasantly surprised. He had been a good friend of Karzai's father, who often told him: if we ever need a new president in Afghanistan, I will support you.

Sattar Sirat was furious after the speech. He saw it as a confirmation of what he had told Brahimi earlier: the Rome Group counted for nothing at the table. He didn't even believe Karzai was really in Uruzgan. This all looks too slick, he thought. It must be staged. Karzai's voice was simply coming from a tape. Sirat gave his first press conference the following day. He didn't mention Karzai's candidacy.

*   *   *

WHILE MANY IN Germany didn't really believe he was in Uruzgan, that was in fact exactly where Karzai was. And he was extremely busy. Some nights he only slept for three hours – he had too many phone calls to make and too many people to receive in his *kala*. He needed to go to Kandahar City with as big a force as possible, to the only remaining Taliban stronghold. All over the province the elders and their men were pressed to join Karzai. It was a lot easier now than it had been a few weeks ago. He also recruited large numbers of ex-Taliban. Most of them were granted immediate amnesty but he no longer sent them home. Instead he tried to keep them close in order to take them to Kandahar later on. In exchange for supporting

Karzai, they received shelter – a roof over their heads in Tarin Kot, with family, with friends, with strangers, with anyone. Those who had been with Karzai from the start frowned on the newcomers. Where were they just a few weeks ago? Back then most people could barely overcome their fear long enough to answer the knock on the door when Karzai or his messenger came calling. Now, six weeks later, everything had changed.

* * *

KARZAI'S HALF-BROTHER AHMAD Wali coordinated the new administration of the other provinces from Quetta.[111] Except for Kandahar, all the southern provinces now seemed to be in Karzai's hands, and were being coordinated by members of his clan. During the Soviet occupation and the civil war their authority was decidedly weakened due to their corrupt behaviour, but that time was over. Ahmad Wali tried to send former government leaders, who were driven out by the Taliban, back to their regions. They had to organise their own support there and assume their former positions. Just as the American Special Forces handed out money in Uruzgan without having to account for any of it, Ahmad Wali also handed out large amounts of dollars, rupees, and telephones. Unlike the Americans, he wrote down precisely what he handed out: this one got US$80,000, that one US$10,000, another received US$50,000. He determined the amounts himself.

Sher Mohammed Akhundzada was one of those provincial leaders. His father, the previous governor of neighbouring Helmand Province and a notorious drug dealer, had been killed during the Taliban regime. Before 9/11, Sher Mohammed Akhundzada tried to take action from Quetta and he accompanied Karzai regularly to the U.S. Embassy in Islamabad to ask for help.[112] It was only after the attacks on the Twin Towers that the U.S. answered their pleas. At Ahmad Wali's urging, when he went from Quetta to his home province of Helmand, he dropped by Karzai in Tarin Kot. Karzai gave him more money. "And if you need the Americans, let me know," Karzai offered. Akhundzada laughed scornfully. "I won't be needing them," he had said. First he liberated the Kajaki Lake, and then he took the city of Musa Kala, followed by the capital city Lashkar Gah. Taliban resistance was easily broken, many of them ceding their power to the returning government officials in exchange for amnesty.

Beyond the borders of the Pashtun region the Taliban didn't have it as easy. In large areas of Afghanistan, Northern Alliance militants and other warlords were on the hunt for the last remaining Arabs, Pakistanis, and Taliban. They had additional incentives: the CIA was handing out a reward for every captured al-Qaeda operative, the first – together with a lot of Afghans—to be taken to the prison at Guantánamo Bay in Cuba. The Taliban were in essence outlaws, on the run from the new rulers.[113] They moved across the country like shadows, trying to stay out of enemy hands. They knew that surrendering to the Northern Alliance meant certain death. The United Nations and the Red Cross weren't options, either. They and other international organisations claimed they had neither the space nor the capacity to take in the group. A representative of the Red Cross did fly to America to ask for a more humane treatment of the Taliban refugees, but the U.S. Army didn't want to hear it. The regime, so hated by the West, couldn't count on any help.

For many Talibs, Karzai seemed to be the safest alternative. Just how much Karzai was willing to accommodate them was demonstrated when Taliban commander Mullah Dadullah surrendered. The one-legged Pashtun from Char Chino district in Uruzgan was a prominent and cruel commander of the Taliban. After September 11 he fought the Northern Alliance and the Americans as long as possible. When the Taliban forces collapsed, he wanted protection, intending to return to the south, and sought out a new ally in his enemy, the Uzbek general Rashid Dostum. Dostum had recently driven the Taliban from territory and together with the Americans he was back in "his" city of Mazar-e-Sharif. Dadullah made a quick deal with Dostum and received safe passage to Kandahar on condition that he delivered a few Arabs to Dostum, who would in turn hand them over to the CIA for cash.

When Dadullah finally arrived in his home province, he didn't go directly to Karzai. He preferred to play it the Afghan way, via a trusted fellow tribesman, and so he contacted Hashem Khan, the mighty Ghilzai elder who had previously brought two districts over to Karzai's side. He had been helpful before with surrendering Taliban to Karzai. He took Mullah Dadullah to Karzai, where everything was quickly arranged.[114] Karzai gave him a letter of safe conduct and he left for Quetta. He joined the other Taliban leaders in exile. One by one the anti-Taliban insurgents like the Lion of Kandahar, Gul Agha Sherzai, former Helmand administrator Sher Mohammed Akhundzada, and of course Karzai himself were leaving the city, while the Taliban were now using Quetta as their base.

Although one Taliban combatant after another was granted amnesty, not everyone was so lucky. Karzai chased personal rivals the moment he got the opportunity. When Karzai was airlifted to Jacobabad in Pakistan, he had already agreed with the Americans on how they could take Mullah Shafiq down.[115] Mullah Shafiq was a prominent Taliban leader from Uruzgan, but, more then that, he was a decades long rival of the Popolzais like Jan Mohammed. (Jan Mohammed told me was confident it was Mullah Shafiq who put him in prison, as another act in this longstanding feud). That's why Shafiq had to pay the price now: not because of his different ideas on religion and women rights but because of enmity. The Americans who had no idea about the real reasons of this kill-mission were happy to use the eager Barakzai Rozi Khan, who knew Shafiq well. They lived close together, and they worked together during the war against the Soviets. Rozi Khan loaned Shafiq empty houses for his fighters and in return Rozi Khan could always count on Shafiq for the same. But with the rise of the Taliban, Rozi Khan was marginalised while his friend Shafiq worked his way up the ranks of the Taliban.

In preparation for an air-attack on Shafiq, Rozi Khan gathered his fighters and the Americans provided the appropriate equipment to direct the bomber jets. The U.S. commandos had their Afghan clothing on, wearing long shirts over their uniforms. Their army trousers could still be seen underneath, and the Americans didn't exactly look authentic. Some of them had tried to wind turbans around their heads, but couldn't quite get the hang of it. Others didn't even bother, and left their baseball caps on. They drove to the stronghold of the feared Shafiq. As they got closer Rozi Khan pointed to a *kala*. Without an interpreter Karzai was the only link between the Afghans and Amerine, so at every instruction Rozi Khan grabbed the telephone to call Karzai, passing the message through him and then handing the telephone to the Americans. "That's it" said Rozi Khan. "That is his house, you can go ahead and bomb it." With a few well-aimed rockets, Shafiq's house was levelled, but Shafiq himself had already fled to Quetta.

*   *   *

WHILE KARZAI REPEATEDLY called for a *loya jirga* for all of Afghanistan, where every elder could participate, it didn't happen in Uruzgan, because the leadership in the province was already divided and there was little left to talk about. In the end the Barakzai and the Popolzai, the very same tribes who dominated before the Taliban, held most of the power in Uruzgan. The mighty pro-Karzai men from other tribes, such as Hashem Khan, were left out; despite Hashem Khan's help for Karzai, his tribe was still a problem. But the Popolzai and Barakzai influence didn't reach everywhere in the province. In the north and east several areas were left alone. They didn't pay much attention to those remote districts either. Karzai and his commandos had only one objective: to get to Kandahar city.

ELEVEN

Carnival in Kandahar: The Race to the Last Taliban Stronghold

WHEN KARZAI'S CONVOY left Tarin Kot, the Afghans were elated. They had only one objective: Kandahar, the Taliban's governing city. Old painted "jingle trucks" were festooned with shiny little silver bells, and some drivers had even placed speakers on the roofs of their vehicles so they could drive triumphantly along the Uruzgan mountain passes playing loud Afghan music. Drivers all tried to position their vehicles as close as possible to Karzai's, to show their support. The convoy zigzagged up and down the mountains. Buses, jeeps, tractors, trucks with farmers and market stall owners looking for a change of scenery, were all on the move. The American fighter jets in direct communication with the Americans in the convoy flew above the messy procession. Elders who hadn't yet been given positions in the province's new administration also followed the new leader.

Amerine was at the front of the convoy, seated in the back of a dilapidated green jeep. The image that their convey brought to mind was of a carnival. He'd never seen anything like it. Chaos, enthusiasm, turbans everywhere, and even men riding along on donkeys. The only person not allowed to come along—Karzai had forbidden it – was the new governor, the 6 foot 1 inches tall Mualim Rahmatullah. They were already at the Tarin Kot airfield when Karzai stopped him. "You need to take care of Uruzgan while we're gone," Karzai told him. "If we need anything, we'll call."

Said was also in the convoy, somewhere in the middle, with the men who had been with Karzai from the start. He had travelled this road so often during the past couple of weeks to arrange matters for Karzai, and here he was again. Everyone had thought Said had been killed in the battle of Tarin Kot. They had asked about him a couple of times, but they never found any sign that he had survived. After his run-in with the Taliban, Said had taken off. On his way he almost walked right into the American airstrike. He was near the road where hundreds of Taliban had thundered past. Bombs had been falling everywhere and Said finally found shelter and safety with an acquaintance. This was where he heard about the return of Karzai to Tarin Kot. He didn't hesitate for a second and ran barefoot straight to Karzai's *kala*, his feet so cut up from running in the mountains that he could no longer stand to wear his slippers. The reunion with Karzai was emotional. "Where are the men you had with you?" Karzai asked. Said lied to him. "Arrested," he said, although he actually suspected they were dead. By now it was clear to him that the Taliban era was over and so he brought up his ambitions to become mayor of the city. But Karzai told him he had already given the position to someone else and that there was no place for him in the city's administration. Said was angry and even yelled at Karzai: "You are a stupid person, and I don't want to see you anymore" and he slammed the *kota* door behind him. Said saw that Karzai followed him immediately and offered Said 200,000 rupees (US$3,200). And so Said joined the convoy.

Signs of the past weeks' battle could be seen all along the road to Kandahar. Jeeps like crushed cans, lifted by the force of explosions, thrown into mountainsides, their carcasses later stripped of anything of value. Every few yards there was an elongated mound of sand, sometimes with a flag. Apparently a few men still had the courage to bury their comrades' bodies along the side of the road. Amerine had no time to reflect. He had to stay alert in case of unexpected attacks.

Halfway to Kandahar they set up camp once again. They needed to wait for another drop of weapons, ammunition, and food. In the hamlet of Petawak they checked into a *caravanserai*, a kind of nomad hotel where the hundreds of fighters barely fit. Karzai immediately took to the street. Ever the politician, he walked around, waving, shaking hands. A stream of children approached him. Everyone already seemed to know him here. Major Bolduc, watching him closely, realised the word-of-mouth promotion had even reached this hole in the wall. The same would happen in his hometown Laconia, he thought to himself. If a stranger were to walk into the local Dunkin Donuts there, everyone would know it.

That evening they received a transmission from CIA agent Graig about a new Taliban attack. Sixteen cars were on their way to Petawak. Karzai immediately sent a few armed men to meet them. Seven cars with Taliban were forced to stop and the men were detained and disarmed. Instantly they switched to Karzai's side. When everything was quiet and Karzai called Mualim Rahmatullah, the new Uruzgan governor. "Bring eggs, bring mutton, bring everything you have—we're hungry," he told him. It was past sundown and the Afghans were allowed to eat again. Rahmatullah was eager to carry out the order – it would give him the opportunity to join the victory convoy.

Ramadan was beginning to affect the Americans. For days they had tried to adapt to the strict fasting schedule. Amerine believed it was important to show respect to the Afghans. But they couldn't handle the day-long fasting any more, and turned to their MREs – "Meals Ready to Eat"— of rice with Stroganoff sauce or a vegetarian chili.

Meanwhile the helicopters with the weapons and food had arrived. This time private mail – a first—was delivered along with their supplies. The Americans had only been in the region for two weeks but the letters were a welcome change. Some commandos had written to their families prior to leaving for Uruzgan to tell them that they wouldn't see them before Christmas.

*   *   *

THAT SAME EVENING, while all eyes were on Kandahar, the political circus on the Petersberg in Germany came to Karzai. The U.N. conference in the luxury hotel had been underway for almost a week now, yet little progress had been made. When the men in the *caravanserai* saw Karzai on the phone with Germany, they watched tensely. Would he be told he was Afghanistan's new leader and that therefore their futures would be rosy from this day forward? Karzai had a surprising answer for them, though. The decision had come through: Sattar Sirat, he told his men, would head Afghanistan's new government.

The tension in the *kala* could be cut with a knife as everyone sat silently taking in the announcement.[116] Sattar Sirat? Not Karzai? Wasn't he going to go to Kabul? Didn't he just speak to the conference in Germany a few days ago on the telephone? Everyone in the *kala* had been confident that the interim presidency was in the bag. The Sirat decision came from nowhere. They hadn't even reached Kandahar city, and now it seemed Karzai's presidency had been taken from them. "I will be the second man," Karzai told them. The usually relaxed and jolly police chief Aziz yelled so loudly that the other men jumped: "Sirat isn't a Pashtun and he hasn't lived in Afghanistan for years! He's an Uzbek." Aziz, who had had so much trouble with the Taliban in recent years, saw all their plans falling apart. Karzai didn't say much. Aziz saw that he intended to accept the Bonn decision and go straight to Kabul to report for his future as vice president.

Karzai suggested calling one of his best Taliban connections, army leader Mullah Naqibullah from Kandahar. Karzai had kept in touch with him while the Taliban were in power. After September 11 he arranged a satellite telephone for him, hoping it would enable access to the Taliban and become a source of information. Karzai thought he would be a suitable governor of Kandahar province once he was in charge, and he suggested that Naqibullah could take over his mission if he had to go to Kabul. The men from Uruzgan strongly disagreed and thought Karzai should still aim for the presidency. "If you don't, I'll give myself up to the Taliban," Aziz cried. "So do something. Call the king, now!" The men themselves also began to call various people, among them some of the participants at the conference in Germany. They had become more comfortable with the satellite telephones, and had them all flipped open. From their small elongated *kala* they tried to turn the tide.

At that same time, in Bonn, Qayyum Karzai was frustrated as well. Qayyum was Hamid Karzai's older brother and the spitting image of his younger sibling. The last couple of years he had lived in America, where he built up his own restaurant chain, "The Helmand." In addition, he represented the family in talks with the State Department, the CIA, and the Pentagon. He was at the conference as an advisor to the Rome Group, and to his dismay he saw how his brother's plans shattered. The Afghans had been talking for a week now, fasting during the day, and exhaustion was taking its toll. Foreign diplomats tried to stick to the fasting schedule, which was made much easier by the Afghans' schedule. They slept in quite late during the day, and the real talks and meetings took place primarily in the evenings and at night.

According to Qayyum, Sirat had manipulated the outcome by promising other members of the Rome Group ministerial positions if they voted for him.[117] The warlord

Pacha Khan Zadran was one of them. After the vote, a guilty look on his face, he walked over to the chairman and said in a loud voice "Sirat told me to vote for him in return for a ministerial position for my brother. And now I've betrayed Karzai!" It was obvious to Qayyum that the proceedings were a joke, that Afghans couldn't handle democracy. "It's sadistic to suddenly expect a child that can't even walk on its own to run," he said in an interview.

Still, the result was clear-cut: eleven votes for Sirat, two for Karzai, and one for Amin Arsala. A few delegation members immediately congratulated Sirat, while others looked on uneasily. It wasn't long before news of the outcome reached the other conference participants. Within five minutes everyone in the hotel knew: Rome had chosen Sirat, an Uzbek.

A brief panic ensued. The plan to launch Karzai as president had apparently failed. The Americans at the conference immediately wondered if it was wise to give these old monarchists the privilege of choosing Afghanistan's new leader. If the decision held, it would undoubtedly cause problems with the other members of the delegation, and especially with the current president, Rabbani, who was already proudly seated in Kabul and who would definitely not be willing to step down for an Uzbek. The Northern Alliance representatives, still in Kabul, were immediately on the phone. "This is a disaster, undo the decision, undo it immediately," Abdullah Abdullah cried over the phone.[118]

For a while the U.N.'s top man, Brahimi, was at a loss. The other conference participants tried everything to change the Rome Group's and Sirat's minds. The first to make an attempt was Zalmay Khalilzad, an Afghan and a naturalised American citizen who worked for the National Security Council. But the Rome Group claimed he had been lobbying for Karzai for months. Sirat remained obstinate. "I didn't create this problem. You'll just have to figure it out. I never agreed with the idea that it should be a Pashtun. I was opposed to the ethnic division of Afghanistan. We are Afghans and there's your choice."

Next it was the chairman's turn. Yunus Qanuni of the Northern Alliance, a slight man with a limp, had already been promised minister of internal affairs. Yet when the international diplomats in attendance asked him to persuade Sirat to give way to Karzai, he unexpectedly said: "It's fine, choose Sirat, it's a good choice."[119] The Westerners were shocked. Now even the Northern Alliance appeared to be dropping Karzai, The reason for Qanuni's decision, as it turned out, was fairly prosaic. He was Sirat's brother-in-law.

In exasperation the king in Rome was called by his cabinet chief. The king typically stayed in the background. Now he had to show his colours. "Matters are not going well, Your Highness," his cabinet chief said to him over the phone. Zahir Shah would not choose an approach that often led to serious arguments between opposing groups, something the Rome Group had seen all too often. This time was no different.[120] The cabinet chief didn't let up. "You have to choose because it must be a Pashtun—that was the agreement." The king claimed to know nothing about any such agreement and hung up. A lengthy phone call with Brahimi was equally unproductive. But a little later the king's cabinet chief got another call. "Choose Karzai', the king said. "He's like a son to me. He's the only one of you actually in Afghanistan."

They debated with Sirat for hours before he finally accepted the king's wishes. He was furious and saw conspiracies at work. "Brahimi is an American puppet," he shouted. "The CIA is behind this." He was deeply offended that he and his Rome Group weren't informed earlier about the existing agreement concerning Karzai. The conference's German hosts were finally able to change his mind. They pointed out that the conference was taking a long time and that they also had to write a new constitution. And the situation in Kabul was getting very ugly. Northern Alliance troops had already committed gruesome murders and they had to be stopped. Finally Sirat said he didn't wish to delay the process any longer. A couple of days later Khalilzad offered him a choice of three key positions in the new administration: chief justice of the Afghan Supreme Court, vice president in combination with the ministry of justice, or chairman of the yet to be established committee of the *loya jirga* which to be held in Kabul after Karzai's appointment. Sirat refused all of them.

Karzai received the nomination after all. He heard the news from Rabbani, who was still in the presidential palace in Kabul. "I'm thinking of you as the next president," he told Karzai. "I could agree to hand over my position to you. What do you think?"[121] Karzai told the men accompanying him to Kandahar about the phone call from Rabbani. He hesitated again. "Should I do it?" he asked them. They shook their heads in disbelief. Aziz spoke first. "Of course you should do it! How can you doubt it?" he shouted at Karzai. Karzai was hesitant and he grabbed the telephone to call Rome for advice. Only after another small meeting with the men did he accept. They breathed a collective sigh of relief. Karzai had taken a decision.

While the conference participants continued to talk in Germany, Karzai and his men continued on to Kandahar city. It was slow going. To the Americans' annoyance, the line of cars and everything surrounding it kept stopping because the Afghans wanted to pray. Five times a day, and it wasn't up for debate. At first it gave the Americans a bit of a scare when the caravan suddenly stopped. Was it a tactical hole, an enemy group that they overlooked that suddenly showed up? They eventually adjusted and accepted the delays. When the Afghans bowed their bodies deep toward Mecca, the commandos surrounded them to guarantee their safety. Then it was quiet for a moment. Some men muttered prayers, many others were quiet and closed their eyes. When the prayers were over, they started moving again.

Amerine was at the front of the convoy, along with the men from Deh Rawud. They were led by the thirty-something-year old Bari Gul (a.k.a. "Flower of the Creator") of the Babozai tribe, to which the Taliban ruler Mullah Omar had strong ties. Two of Omar's wives were members of this tribe. Gul was also one of the seven who was invited by Karzai to Quetta in the early days. He was the son of a renowned commander from Deh Rawud. At home he often played in the belly of a downed Soviet helicopter. It was hung like a swing in the *kala*. He wanted to follow in his father's footsteps and become a heroic warrior.

When the caravan reached Shah Wali Kot, Amerine, Gul and about thirty men left the convoy to take advance positions. The verdant Shah Wali Kot district is the bridge between Kandahar and Uruzgan, an area with mud brick villages surrounded by lush farmland, orchards, and rivers. But it was not exactly peaceful yet. That same evening Amerine and Gul were caught in a skirmish with about thirty to fifty Taliban. American air power had bombed the convoy's route every night, and this was their first direct confrontation on the ground. Amerine was on a mountain ridge right outside a village, together with Gul and his men. He emptied his magazine at the enemy. Out of the corner of his eye Amerine saw that his Afghans were running away. He was frustrated. "Again," he thought, "again they bow out!" He reloaded his weapon and fired. To his dismay, he had used a magazine of tracer rounds. Suddenly Gul and the Americans were sitting ducks in the bright light. The Taliban, who up to that point had hardly been able to hit anything in the dark, now fired a volley at Amerine and his men, who scrambled to get behind the ridge. After a few confusing minutes they recovered and fired back. They yelled at the communications sergeant: "No air support, no air support!" It was only a hamlet and Amerine didn't want to risk civilian casualties by bombing the place. When the greatly diminished Taliban group finally fled, Amerine had a brief sense of victory. Quickly they moved into the first hamlet. It was the first step to

Kandahar city.

Shah Wali Kot was no longer completely in Taliban hands. Some parts had been taken over by local insurgents, like the hamlet of Damana, where Karzai found lodgings at a safe distance from the fighting. The future president walked around somewhat aimlessly. All he could do now was wait. He enjoyed it, though. After the past few weeks behind the high walls of safe houses in Tarin Kot, now at least he could go outside. One of Damana's residents gave him a small mattress on which to sit. No playing children welcomed the leader this time. Large groups of Afghans refugees passed by, primarily women and children fleeing the fighting between Karzai's men and the Taliban.

The convoy's advance group reached a dry river-bed by a bridge that evening, about eighteen miles from Kandahar city. About a hundred Taliban attacked from across the bridge and especially from one orchard with low walls. Amerine fired illumination flares in order to determine the enemy's position. Several of his Afghan fighters fled. He knew he couldn't fight the Taliban without help, so he requested air support. The Taliban group across the bridge were bombarded all night long. From the convoy they could see trails of light and explosions. Everything was crushed: houses, shops, and sheep pens collapsed, and the trees in the orchards were aflame.

Afterwards, once everything had settled down, the Americans found Karzai and took him to Shah Wali Kot. The moment he entered the district, he called his Taliban friend Mullah Naqibullah again. He had spoken with Karzai frequently on the phone in recent weeks to update him about the movements of the Taliban.[122] He had also tried to convince the Taliban—on Karzai's behalf—not to fight. Since Hamid Karzai was getting closer to victory, over the following days Naqibullah would be instrumental in brokering contacts between the Taliban and Karzai. Naqibullah had already received a phone call from the Taliban about their desire to surrender. But later they had changed their mind, Naqibullah told Karzai. But I will try to see them again, he promised.

The next day Karzai's men started off in a good mood. They had a leisurely breakfast before they started another long day of fasting. They were positioned near the village of Said Alim Kalay. Three thousand men of Karzai's fighting force were spread out all over the place. Karzai was busily talking to CIA agent Graig and some Afghans.[123] Haji Bahadur (The Hero) from Deh Rawud was also present and everyone thanked him for the stunt he pulled the evening before when he entered the battle with a confiscated Taliban truck. They were discussing how they could get back the bodies of the six men he lost, taken by the Taliban.

Suddenly there was an enormous explosion. Haji Bahadur was thrown on the floor and only heard buzzing in his ears. He couldn't see anything in the room where he was talking with Karzai and Graig. All the windows were shattered and dust clouds drifted in. He tried to find Karzai and then saw his bloody face.

A few hours before the explosion new commandos were flown in, among them a 'Joint Terminal Attack Coordinator' or JTAC, a soldier who passes on the coordinates of enemy targets to the bomber jets.[124] In order to take out the last Taliban forces across the riverbed, the JTAC called for air support around 9:30 a.m. But something had gone horribly wrong. A 1,000 kg satellite-guided JDAM bomb, dropped from a B-52 plane, fell precisely on the spot where Karzai and his men were spread out over the mountain.

After the strike cries of pain could be heard all around. The valley was filled with a thickening black cloud. The force of the explosion had thrown Amerine to the ground and for a moment he didn't understand what had happened. When he tried to get up he saw how much damage the bomb had done. Everyone on the mountain was shouting. "What happened, what's going on?" Suddenly there were dead men all around them. Amerine quickly counted dozens of fallen fighters. Horribly marred bodies were scattered everywhere. And blood—there was blood everywhere. Bari Gul's group from Deh Rawud was hit the hardest. They never left Amerine's side and hardly any of them had survived. Bari Gul's face was half blown off by the explosion. The euphoria and elation during the departure from Tarin Kot had now evaporated. "What do we do?" Amerine wondered.

Soon the sound of the rescue helicopters reached them. Some of the most heavily wounded Afghans were carried to the choppers. Karzai lay in the dust. He was lucky, even though he had a head wound—a shell-splinter near his eye. The Americans immediately took him to another mountain top for treatment. The rest stayed behind. In a daze Amerine walked through the devastation and tried to help as many of the wounded as possible. When he directed his

A-team to the helicopters he discovered that two of the eleven are missing. It turned out one of the men in Bolduc's C-team was killed as well. Before he knew it, Amerine himself was on his way to Germany, to Landstuhl military hospital at Ramstein, the US air base. He wasn't seriously wounded, but his eardrums were damaged and he had bomb fragments in his leg. He arrived ahead of his fallen friends. A special forensic team following the troops had to first identify them based on what was left of their bodies.

The Afghans literally didn't know what had hit them.[125] Some had heard that al-Qaeda launched a rocket from Kandahar Airport, but Karzai and CIA agent Graig admitted it was an American mistake. The mistake was made by a woman, they said. "Because she didn't have much experience yet with Afghanistan", they told Haji Bahadur. The men didn't believe it. Still it remained unclear to them what had happened.

There was more bad news. Karzai heard Gul Agha Sherzai was getting close to Kandahar from the south. Sherzai also had the support of an American A-team and was now moving on the city at high speed. Because Sherzai was operating on his own, Karzai tried to stop him by threatening him in various ways. Sherzai wasn't listening.

While the Lion of Kandahar moved on the city centre, the U.N. conference thousands of miles away in Germany was ceremoniously concluded, after much faltering and floundering. Ministerial posts were fought over in the hotel on the Petersberg until the wee hours of the night. President Rabbani wasn't prepared to step down after all, and he demanded much more authority. He only agreed to give in after a rocket "accidentally" exploded next to his home in Kabul.[126] The number of ministerial posts rose to twenty-nine. Only then would the Northern Alliance accept Karzai's interim presidency. When the conference was over, Karzai received a call from an acquaintance, the BBC reporter Lyse Doucet. "You are the new leader of Afghanistan," she said. Karzai reacted as if this is the first he had heard of it.[127]

Kandahar city was being besieged on two sides, and the Taliban realised their last stronghold wouldn't hold much longer. They approached Mullah Naqibullah again. In a two-day deliberation the remaining Taliban rulers—about ten of them—discussed the situation. Naqibullah joined one meeting, hosted in a foreign NGO in the hope that the building wouldn't be bombed. Naqibullah noticed the absence of Mullah Omar, but the Taliban assured him they were speaking on his behalf. Some of the members of the meeting had always had good relations with Karzai, like Mullah Abdul Salam "Rocketi", who got his nickname during the war against the Soviets. He was one of the top three commanders of the military branch of the Taliban and he ruled eastern Nangarhar province. He had been driven out a few days earlier, and surrendered to Karzai in Uruzgan via a messenger and returned to his home region near Kandahar.[128]

Mullah Abdul Razzaq and Mullah Khairulla Khairkhwa also attended the Taliban-meeting. Both were well-known Popolzai who had been in contact with Karzai for years. Mullah Baradar, the prominent Taliban commander from

Uruzgan and a fellow tribesman of Karzai's, was also present.

The atmosphere of the deliberations was tense since the Taliban were divided.[129] Some wanted to continue fighting, others refused. After a daylong heated debate, they decided to surrender. Mullah Naqibullah, the go-between, was asked to contact Karzai in Shah Wali Kot.

When Naqibullah returned with the message that they could talk, a delegation was sent, led by Mullah Omar's second in command, Mullah Obaidullah Akhund. He was minister of defence and in charge of communications between the Taliban and the Pakistani secret service, more commonly known as the ISI. The delegation left, accompanied by, among others, Mullah Omar's brother-in-law. The Taliban leaders were freed and would support Karzai.

While Kandahar would become Karzai's after a peace deal with the Taliban, the Americans intervened. First, Karzai wasn't allowed to see the Taliban in Shah Wali Kot. "Don't let them come here," Karzai said over the satellite phone to Naqibullah. But the go-between refused and warned Karzai that the surrender would fail if Karzai was not prepared to meet face-to-face. Ultimately Karzai managed to convince the American soldiers to let him have a meeting in Shah Wali Kot.[130] The moment the first delegation arrived was only 4 or 5 hours after the 'friendly fire' had hit Hamid Karzai and his team. When the delegation approached Hamid Karzai, a helicopter with fresh American soldiers landed and they pointed their weapons at the Taliban. The son of Naqibullah saw what happened. "Before a shooting could start, Karzai's men made a sign with their fingers, which meant: these are good people, please let us go. Then the Americans let us go." Karzai retreated with the delegation, along with some trusted men from Uruzgan, like Rozi Khan, Aziz Agha and Abdul Rahim Akhundzada.[131] The talks of surrender were extensive and Karzai's men knew that this would be one of the most important moments on their journey to power.[132] Karzai asked Akhundzada to search the Taliban before they entered the room, but Akhundzada knew Obaidullah, Mullah Abdul Razzaq, Mullah Akhtar Mohammed Akhund, Tayyeb Agha and Rais-e Bagran. "They were trusted man", Akhundzada would later recall. "It would have been an insult to search them."[133]

The delegation had a letter from Mullah Omar, Karzai said. "Mullah Omar stated that, considering the decision of the U.N. conference, he accepted me as the new leader." But others who attended the meeting disagree with Karzai on the letter. According to Akhundzada, the delegation showed a letter that Mullah Omar had written. But it wasn't a letter of surrender, according to Akhundzada. "Mullah Omar had written: 'It's up to the cabinet to decide about what will happen with the transition of power.'" Aziz Agha confirmed this. It was clear that Mullah Omar didn't wanted to transfer power directly. But according to his men, in the end, Karzai accepted the proposal. Then they talked about handing over the weapons and vehicles to Mullah Naqibullah. One of Karzai's men said: hand over the money, we want to have the power and the money. But Obaidullah declined. "He said everything is gone; we survive on potatoes", according to Akhundzada. They then talked about ending the American air strikes on Kandahar city, which Karzai promised to arrange. In turn, Karzai demanded that the Taliban confirm on the radio that they had surrendered and that the fighting in the city must therefore stop.

In addition, Karzai strongly urged that the Taliban's prisoners be freed. He was particularly concerned about one man, Jan Mohammed, his old ally from Tarin Kot who was governor of Uruzgan prior to the Taliban regime. He had Karzai's trust, as well as that of several of the fighters Karzai had gathered around himself in Uruzgan over the past few months. Jan Mohammed was seen as a fearless warrior, and Karzai really didn't want to go to Kandahar without him. The Taliban had surrendered, it was true, but still, who knew what could happen? The city was in chaos. When the delegation was leaving, Taliban minister Obaidullah personally promised to send bread for the night. He later sent 2500 pieces of bread, according to Aziz Agha. Obaidullah also recognised that Kandahar wasn't safe for Karzai yet. "There are some Arab and Pakistanis among the Taliban", he told Aziz Agha. "If you are attacked, don't get mad, because we don't want that. We don't want to attack you, but there are Arabs and Pakistanis who do. Please don't think that we did it."

The Taliban delivered Jan Mohammed shortly afterwards, as arranged. Mullah Obaidullah was with them. They arrived in an old Toyota Corolla. Miraculously, Jan Mohammed had been kept alive through his time in Taliban prison, but Karzai and his men were appalled. They hardly recognised their old leader. His complexion was pale and sickly from lack of sunlight. His body was emaciated and his beard was filthy, long, and grey. As Jan Mohammed walked toward Karzai he yelled: "Kill all the Taliban. Kill them all!" Karzai immediately took his friend aside and informed him in a long meeting what had been agreed. Then a new problem arose. When Karzai said he wanted to leave at once, Jan Mohammed objected. He needed to go to Tarin Kot. "My family thinks I'm dead," he told them. "I have to report home first." Karzai, who was about to take the last step in this war, would have to wait one more day. The following morning Jan Mohammed returned with almost one hundred cars full of armed men and he joined the others on the road to Kandahar city.

Kandahar was indeed a city in chaos. Naqibullah had arranged his governorship of Kandahar province with Karzai. But while Naqibullah was taking territory district-by-district with the help of a prominent Talib Gul Agha, his work was suddenly interrupted. Sherzai's men started fighting Mullah Naqibullah's troops. Clearly, Sherzai didn't agree with the surrender of Kandahar and was trying to become governor himself. It became a game between Karzai and his American backers entering Kandahar from the North, and on the other side Gul Agha Sherzai who stormed the city with a different team of Americans. Sherzai together with his American supporters said in the media that "Mullah Naqib is working with the Arabs and is Taliban." Sherzai knew at that time that Naqibullah wasn't a Talib any more. Before 9/11, they had met each other in opposition meetings in Pakistan to fight the Taliban. But at that moment, the truth wasn't convenient for Sherzai. He managed to convince his Americans that Naqibullah was their enemy and he had to be defeated. He said to the Americans: "He won't help you hunt Taliban: he'll help them against you."[134] Naqibullah responded emotionally. "Go and check me, go and check my house, whatever you want to know. I am not a Talib."[135] But it was too late. Karzai wasn't able to stop Sherzai and his US-team. When Karzai was on the phone with Sherzai he insulted Karzai. "I don't know who Hamid Karzai is, and I don't know Mullah Naqib. Kandahar is mine."[136] Soon the peace deal Karzai had made with the Taliban evaporated. The son of Naqibullah had to flee his house with his father, he says, because the Americans wanted to kill Naqibullah. In panic, Karzai had called his father and said: leave your house, the Americans will bomb it very soon. It was clear for Naqibullah that the surrender of Kandahar was a lost cause.

The new president of Afghanistan already had lost one of the most important cities of the country. The Americans didn't want to believe in a peace deal and a quiet surrender of the most significant city in Afghanistan. Though the US diplomats and generals should have done their homework, not many Americans knew how Afghans always make deals. Karzai was always in contact with certain Talibs (as with Massoud's people and Hizb-e Islami) and knew how to play Pashtun politics. Though Karzai was now the president and the boss of the country, the Americans overruled him. Gul Agha Sherzai used the US' anti-Taliban sentiment by telling them what they wanted to hear, and in doing so took power himself.

After this debacle, Karzai prepared himself for his first

interviews as Afghanistan's new interim president. CNN reporter Christiane Amanpour arrived in a jeep adorned with I LOVE NEW YORK stickers and got first dibs.[137]

Events began to take on momentum. Karzai boarded an American helicopter that would take him to Kabul. He only took a few people, although all his men would have liked to come along to the capital city to protect him against the Northern Alliance. Karzai refused, and sent everyone back to Uruzgan. He didn't want to give the Alliance the impression he didn't trust them.

Epilogue

D URING OUR FINAL conversation Karzai was seated at a raised wooden desk in the presidential palace in Kabul. A few silver pens lay neatly in a row under the warm light of a green banker's lamp. The table looked immaculate. No mess, no computer, no mail. We spoke at length about "his" men from Uruzgan. "Oooh yes, Ibrahim, he's in Kabul," the president exclaimed. "I still need to ask him something." Karzai grabbed the telephone and got him on the line almost immediately. "How are you—good? When are you going back to Uruzgan?" Ibrahim was appointed governor of a district in Helmand province in 2001 and was now a prominent member of the Provincial Council of Uruzgan.

Karzai told me enthusiastically which important positions he had given his men since 2001. After he had lost Kandahar to a rival who was supported by American Special Forces, Karzai's only alternative was to rely heavily on his own network. As a consequence he had made sure that many other provinces were manned with loyalists, qualified or not. To me it sounded corrupt: Karzai's system was based on favours and patronage. But Karzai didn't feel ashamed at all. He told me he in this situation he could lean on these men. His personal bodyguard Mohammed Shah became head of security and now walked the halls of the presidential palace in his dusty, worn-out shoes. His appointment was to the great chagrin of others for whom it was obvious that Shah had not been appointed because of his qualifications or his training in the security business. He did something for Karzai and so he got something in return. It was no different, as far as Karzai's critics were concerned, from how the other security guards from 2001 got their jobs. Haji Faizullah was with Karzai when they crossed the Afghan border in October 2001 and was currently first secretary at the embassy in Abu Dhabi. His third security guard now had the same position with Karzai's half-brother Ahmad Wali in Kandahar.

Of course, some warriors who were with Karzai from the start felt they were being short-changed when the Karzais were handing out the positions. For instance, they would demand a ministerial post, while Hamid Karzai but also his half-brother Ahmed Wali Karzai believed they were merely suitable for a position as district governor or police chief. Former police chief Aziz had also counted on a ministerial post in Kabul, but had to make do with a position as provincial director of agriculture in Uruzgan. Abdul Ghani Mama, one of the first to offer his hospitality to Karzai at the beginning of the expedition, had expected the governorship of Uruzgan. He was awarded a much more modest position. Ahmad Wali's career, on the other hand, wasn't bad. In the beginning his influence in the south was limited because of Sherzai's presence in Kandahar, but soon he was considered viceroy of the city and in

2005 he was head of the provincial council. Until his death in 2011, he was the king of Kandahar in all but name.

*   *   *

THE WAY KARZAI dealt with 'his' helpers from Uruzgan and Kandahar gives a unique insight into how Karzai and his Afghan and foreign allies try to rule Afghanistan, but aren't able to govern the country.

Following the footprints of the 'helpers' of Karzai answers crucial questions about why the international community and Karzai's government find tremendous difficulties in getting a grip on Afghanistan. What are the reasons for a continuing insurgency? What does corruption mean in Afghanistan?

At the end of 2001, Afghanistan was full of hope for the future. Karzai's promise that everyone would once more be included in governing Afghanistan was well received. As a new leader and fluent speaker of English, he could count on support from the West.

One Taliban-leader after the other had surrendered and gave up fighting to Hamid Karzai. Besides, Hamid Karzai had promised many Taliban they would join the new government.

Soon the American intervention would bring many of them back to the battlefield. Karzai's plan that all the groups – including the Taliban – could join the government didn't come to pass. After he had lost Kandahar to his rival supported by the American Special Forces, any triumph in sight evaporated.

But soon the American intervention would bring many of them back to the battlefield.

In Kabul the power struggle with the other victor in the war – the Northern Alliance – began. In return for supporting Karzai's presidency, the Northern Alliance had received various ministerial posts at the Bonn conference. In July 2002 one of the five vice presidents was killed under questionable circumstances. In addition, Karzai had to deal with various warlords who were – like himself—set aside during the Taliban regime, and who had become powerful again thanks to the American support. The Uzbek anti-Soviet hero Abdul Rashid Dostum demanded a key position in Karzai's administration and was already rebelling against Karzai in 2003.

More then he wanted himself, Karzai needed the leverage of his own people in the Pashtun area.

In Uruzgan, like in so many other provinces, there was also a great inspiration to work all together for a new Afghanistan. Karzai had appointed as governor his fellow warrior and tribesman Mualim Rahmatullah, who at first was generous towards the Taliban in accordance with Karzai's orders. "It was quiet at that point in Uruzgan," Rahmatullah told me. "Nothing serious happened—there were no new Taliban attacks." A few Taliban big wigs were still held prisoner in Tarin Kot and Karzai ordered Rahmatullah to release some of them. "I let every last one walk out of prison. It was a wonderful period. It was peaceful and everything was going to be all right, we were sure of it."

Rahmatullah's reign didn't last long, and neither did

the positive attitude toward the Taliban. A few months after his appointment he was summoned to the presidential palace in Kabul, where he heard that he would be replaced. "The president told me Jan Mohammed would be my successor and that he would give me something else."

The appointment of strongman Jan Mohammed was a sure sign that the attitude toward peace had changed. After all, it was this one eyed man who had yelled "Kill the Taliban, kill the Taliban" after his release from prison in Kandahar city. Similar controversial appointments happened in Helmand and other provinces where Karzai put his friends in the front seat; most of them came with a violent reputation from the civil war. Also, most of them had been at odds with (some of) the Taliban, something they would surely take revenge for. While Human Rights Watch already warned the world about the danger of appointing these men as governors, American soldiers had no problem working with them. Jon Bolduc, the American Special Forces soldier who was also active in Uruzgan when Jan Mohammed came to power spoke of close cooperation between the new governor and the Americans. "We built a very strong relationship with him. We trained his troops and rearmed them so they would be ready to fight the Taliban. The United States empowered them."

The main reason for an increasing insurgency, is that 'their' governors, like Jan Mohammed who were not more then Karzai's political strongmen, became Americans' eyes and ears in the hunt for the Taliban. The amnesty that gave Karzai legitimacy in the early days was already history for the Americans and these local officials who were ready to take revenge. Sometimes Aziz (police commander before the Taliban and now head of Agriculture department) or Jan Mohammed went along with Marines or Special Forces and pointed out houses where ex-Taliban fighters or other enemies were supposed to be. Acting on their advice—'this is Taliban'—the Americans kicked in locked doors and invaded *kotas*.

The American attack on the Taliban in Deh Rawud occurred without Jan Mohammed's approval, but the Americans did it any way. A wedding in Deh Rawud was bombed in the assumption that Mullah Baradar was there. Even though Karzai had granted amnesty in return for a ticket to the palace, that all seemed forgotten now. Mullah Baradar, who continued to believe the amnesty he had been given had been in good faith, stayed in hiding with a good friend and tribesman of Karzai and Jan Mohammed in Deh Rawud. When he saw that the Americans continued to hunt for him, he, too, fled to Pakistan and would become a prominent member of the Taliban-opposition.

In 2001—during his own revolt—Karzai himself warned his A-Team of Amerine about a problem that would soon bring the American army in Afghanistan to a defeat: retribution. Different groups of Afghans would try to convince the trigger-happy Americans with all sorts of nonsense, to gladly use their bombs to eliminate their personal enemy and not 'the Taliban.' When I spoke with him in 2008, Karzai said the Americans were killing too many civilians, because 'they are using the wrong intelligence'. Of course he was right: the American often failed in this country of rivalry to fulfil their duty of care to gather objective information before using their weapons. But at the same time, Karzai didn't criticise his own government staff members who often were the primary source for this wrong information.

To see how the conflict in Afghanistan developed, and how the Taliban rose again, it is worth reviewing the actions of the people who helped Karzai in 2001. There were different ways where people got captured or killed that stirred unrest. While the outside world expected a hunt for the Taliban, the reality on the ground was much more grim. On the one hand, Afghans got betrayed by Americans. Ghulam Nabi Khan, for example, was a powerful elder but had a dispute with Jan Mohammed's group long before the Taliban came to the surface. Now that Jan Mohammed was back in control, many Afghans in Uruzgan could guess what would happen to Ghulam Nabi Khan. Not surprisingly, he was put under suspicion again and feared the governor's influence. It was possible he was active with the Taliban, but after 2001 he was loyal to the new government of Uruzgan. Still, he was the victim of a slur campaign in which Jan Mohammed accused him of being pro-Taliban. He felt so persecuted that he ended up asking for support from the Americans in Uruzgan. But it was a mistake to expect the Americans to be independent in this conflict, since they mostly trusted the governor. When Ghulam Nabi Khan paid a visit to the Special Forces, they immediately detained him. He was taken to Bagram prison near Kabul, Afghanistan's Guantánamo Bay. He was released six months later. After a meeting with president Karzai he disappeared, allegedly to Helmand.

One event that took place north of Tarin Kot is illustrative of the swamp into which the foreign troops were sinking. A dispute arose between Jan Mohammed and Hashem Khan. Hashem Khan had helped Karzai in 2001 with his uprising, and in 2002 Karzai visited him and assured him nobody would touch him. It was soon apparent that Jan Mohammed thought differently when he frequently harassed Hashem Khan, demanding money from him and forcing him to hand over his guns through the disarmament program. When Hashem Khan (who died mysteriously in 2010) finally fled to Kandahar, his area collapsed into disorder, with minor local elders trying to keep their heads above water and failing to resist Jan Mohammed's militias. Jan Mohammed unjustly dismissed this resistance as being stoked by the Taliban, and Karzai and the Americans believed him.

Resistance against Jan Mohammed, and by extension, Karzai, grew year by year. The Taliban Mullah Shafiq, possibly Jan Mohammed's chief adversary, didn't escape the governor's unrestrained lust for dominance, either. Jan Mohammed was convinced it was Mullah Shafiq who put him in prison during the period of Taliban rule. With Karzai's arrival in 2001 it was obvious to Shafiq that he would lose his command to Jan Mohammed. The governor regularly went to the Mirabad Valley with his militias to take strong action against Shafiq and his followers. Instead of trying to solve the old rivalry between Shafiq and Jan Mohammed through mediation, the Americans chose the governor's side, sent their military and supported him in his attacks in Shafiq's area. Dutch diplomats who were stationed in Uruzgan say detainees were covered with burning plastic and that dead bodies were mutilated by driving over them in jeeps. Shafiq's people fled to Pakistan. From Quetta, Shafiq leads the resistance against the new government in Uruzgan and the foreign forces assisting it.

It wasn't just the numerous feuds Jan Mohammed fought so viciously with other elders in Uruzgan that diminished his popularity. His "drug policy" led to resistance in even the lowest layers of society. Uruzgan has traditionally been an important producer of poppies, from which opium, morphine and heroin are made. These poppy crops were a valuable source of income for Jan Mohammed due to the heavy taxes he levied on them. He did this through the district governors. For instance, the governor of Chora district had to cough up the equivalent of US$1.5 million annually. Via a corrupt network of middlemen the duties ended up being paid by small farmers, for whom the poppy crops were often the primary source of income.

As a result, little was left of the initial optimism about the future of post-Taliban Uruzgan. Jan Mohammed's actions had discredited the governorship and by extension his ally Karzai's central government in Kabul. This led to the impression that five years after 2001 Uruzgan was still a hotbed of resistance against the new pro-Western government in Afghanistan. But the resistance didn't only come from ideological Taliban.

* * *

ALTHOUGH URUZGAN IS a small province, lacking great strategic interest, it clearly shows how prominent strongmen gained power, encouraged by the US troops who made them the supreme kings of the area. But the pattern of increased violence can be found in many other provinces as well. In Kandahar province, where the Taliban took power in 1994 and where Karzai's tribes used to have prominent positions before, reconciliation was soon forgotten. American journalist Anand Gopal studied developments in the southern province after 2001 and drew similar conclusions.

> "The Taliban's resurgence in Kandahar post-2001 was not inevitable or preordained. The Taliban—from senior leadership levels down to the rank and file—by and large surrendered to the new government and retired to their homes. But in the early years after 2001, there was a lack of a genuine, broad-based reconciliation process in which the Taliban leadership would be allowed to surrender in exchange for amnesty and protection from persecution. Rather, foreign forces and their proxies pursued an unrelenting drive against former regime members, driving many of them to flee to Pakistan and launch an insurgency."[138]

Gopal studied the case of Mullah Ahmad Shah in the Mushan village cluster of Panjwayi district, an area often reported on as 'Taliban-area'. Shah, a former Taliban official and military commander who had surrendered, was at home in the early months of the Sherzai government. Government officials arrested Shah and some others on charges of having weapons, took them to a Kandahar city NDS prison, and tortured them. Hajji Fazl Muhammad, who led a group of tribal elders from Panjwayi to the city to try to secure their release, recalled the scene at the prison:

> "We met them in jail and saw that their feet were swollen. Their hands and feet had been tied for days, and they told us that the prison guards would roll them around on the ground. They also beat them with cables. [The prisoners] were begging us to tell the guards to just kill them so that they could be put out of their misery."

Shah was kept in custody for about three weeks, until his family members purchased weapons simply to hand over to the authorities to get him freed. But the men were arrested again and Shah's family was forced to sell all of their livestock so they could pay a bribe to the authorities. A short while later, Shah and others were arrested for a third time and held for 44 days, until immense pressure from tribal elders brought about their release. Shah and his brothers soon fled to Pakistan, joined the burgeoning Taliban insurgency, and returned to Panjwayi as Taliban fighters. Today Shah is the head of the Taliban's main court in Mushan. His brothers Qari Allahuddin and Qari Muhammad Sadiq, along with two other siblings, are also Taliban commanders active in Panjwayi.

When I think of President Karzai, I often am reminded of a quote of the old Afghan ruler, Abdur Rahman. Like Karzai, he more or less talked himself into power and managed to get a certain number of important tribesman, religious leaders or businessmen behind him. But by doing that, he became his own prisoner. Abdur Rahman was very well aware that it was group consensus that was the decisive factor in the assumption and maintenance of power, and stressed this in his talks with the British. These methods ensured stability and viability for the system at least for some time. On the downside, they meant implicating the ruler in a mesh of dependencies and coalitions, which considerably reduced his real power.

Rahman to the British: "I can be nobody's friend nor foe; I can take no position nor sign any agreement without the acceptance and consent of the local chieftains."

Karzai is in exactly the same position. Instead of being the 'good ally of the West', Karzai continued to defend 'his' men who, despite their bad reputation, guaranteed him a rather solid power base. These men were Karzai's 'private' security, and that's where he had to put his loyalty, whether he wanted it or not. Even in Karzai's own family, members cheated on ISAF to improve this power base. The internal feuds had started long ago, in the eighties after Karzai's father's step-brother was murdered by another family member whose name was Yar Mohammed (see Chapter 3 for more). In 2009 and 2011 the conflict erupted again. The first mysterious murder was that of Waheed, the son of Yar Mohammed, that was possibly committed by one of the sons of the murdered stepbrother of Hamid Karzai's father.[139] Then in 2011 ISAF raided a house and killed Yar Mohammed himself. First NATO-led forces said they had killed the father of a Talib after they spotted him holding an AK-47 automatic rifle. Karzai's spokesman responded immediately, knowing what was going on: 'The president calls on ISAF to protect civilians rather than killing them.'[140] Soon it would turn out that there was no such thing as 'killed civilians' or 'Taliban'. Karzai's family had deceived ISAF, made them believe in false intelligence in order to get rid of their rival Yar Mohammed.

Based on Karzai's loyalties, it wasn't a surprise that ISAF faced heavy resistance from Karzai when they wanted to fire one of Karzai's corrupt associates. According to the British, Karzai rejected the accusation of corruption of one of his most important strongmen in the South. After a long political crisis, Karzai replaced governor Sher Mohammed Akhundzada, appointed him as a Senator and warned the British that Helmand would fall out of their hands from now on. Within a year, Karzai fired the new more 'clean' governor, under heavy pressure from the same Sher Mohammed Akhundzada who got backing from the US. Speaking to The Times of London, one British diplomat stated: "The president kept on undermining his own governor, it doesn't help what we are doing here."

The Dutch had the same experience. When they want- ed to fire governor Jan Mohammed for the same reasons, Karzai showed his strong preference for patronage instead of being the president for all Afghans. Talking to Karzai, he blamed the Dutch for not understanding governor Jan Mohammed. "The Dutch made their decision after only hearing the stories of a few angry Afghan citizens." Jan Mohammed 'was his best friend', Hamid Karzai said, and was good 'for the political balance.' "We needed them in this phase of the war." Karzai appointed Jan Mohammed as a minister, a clear sign to the Dutch that he would never accept their intervention.

As an illustration of all this, the events that followed Jan Mohammad's departure are telling. Jan Mohammed's successor was Abdul Hakim Munib, who had been deputy minister under the Taliban. During the mid-nineties when Karzai was still open to working with the Taliban, Munib had travelled to the U.S. Embassy in Islamabad with him to ask for support for the Taliban. In October 2001 he surrendered promptly to Karzai. As a governor of Uruzgan, Munib attempted to restore the tribal balance that Jan Mohammed had disturbed. For instance, in Deh Rawud he tried to get some of the Babozai leaders who had been driven out by his predecessor to return. His efforts only worked for a year. His Taliban past was constantly pointed out by Jan Mohammed sympathisers. Jan Mohammed didn't think much of him, he told me bluntly: "He promised us much. He would do this, he would do that. But he's Taliban." The Americans didn't like Munib of what Jan Mohammed told them. They continued to do business with Jan Mohammed; even though he was no longer governor, he still had his own private armies.

Governance in Uruzgan grew increasingly chaotic. Discord developed between the Americans and the Dutch about the weak governor and Jan Mohammed's continuing influence. In 2007 Munib gave up. Disillusioned, he boarded an aircraft with the contents of Uruzgan's treasury under his shirt. The province was broke. Karzai appointed Asadullah Hamdam from neighbouring Zabul province as Munib's successor. "I love Hamdam," Jan Mohammed told me. "He's opposed to the Taliban." Jan Mohammed said this when he had just appointed a friend as a police commander: "Hamdam couldn't do anything without me. Who do you trust—the governor of your region or your father? Your father? I *am* the father of Uruzgan." Hamdam – who became more and more opposed to the Popolzai influence—was sent home in 2010. He was accused of corruption by a Western NGO, and that – at a time of increasing Western accusations of Karzai's corruption—was enough for Jan Mohammed and his people to get him replaced.

But sidelining the informal kingdom of Karzai's strongmen also backfired on NATO, who now and then faced dangerous situations. After Jan Mohammed's removal under Dutch pressure, he ordered his successor Abdul Hakim Munib to retreat from the area and to give the Chora district over to contending elders. It was a typical move in a patronage system—the former governor wanted to show he still had more muscle than his successor. The region subsequently threatened to fall into the hands of local tribes that were hostile toward one another, some of whom did and some of whom didn't sympathise with the Taliban. After a few days the district governor Obaidullah restored order in Chora, but there are indications that the manoeuvre was repeated in 2007. Once again the area was on the brink of falling into the hands of local militias, organised by Jan Mohammed. There were only about sixty Dutch troops in the capital, Chora town, so the Dutch, taken completely by surprise, sent reinforcements from Camp Holland. The Afghans had abandoned all military checkpoints and police stations in the city, and the roughly five hundred new Dutch troops were immediately outnumbered, facing an estimated fifteen hundred local militants, mainly from Deh Rashan and the Mirabad Valley. Thus began the Battle of Chora, reported in the media as a 'battle against the Taliban', but in reality the distinction between friend and foe was completely blurred. The fighting lasted for days and the Dutch received no support from local authorities. They barely made it out alive. Only the local Barakzai leader Rozi Khan helped the Dutch, even though he had been removed as police chief of Uruzgan under Dutch pressure a year earlier, along with Jan Mohammed. Peace was restored in the region and a year later a vote was organised to choose a new administration. Rozi Khan won it by a narrow margin.

Also, in Kandahar, warlord and police highway commander Matiullah (Popolzai and member of Jan Mohammed's family) allegedly attacked ISAF when he thought it necessary. In summer 2009, relations soured after the Dutch suspected him of being involved in an attack on one of their convoys on the road from Uruzgan to Kandahar. There have been regular allegations that in his role as the de facto and only protector of the Kandahar-Uruzgan highway, Matiullah sometimes creates fake enemies and fake clashes in order to stay in business and to keep the price of security high. While media reported 'Taliban-attacks' against ISAF supported by Karzai's government, there were actually different stories on the ground. On the day the Dutch drove the road without his protection, Matiullah had an interest to attack, since the Dutch refused to pay US 3000 per truck for a secure trip and tried to go on their own. Half-way dozens of land mines exploded and seven Dutch soldiers were wounded.

The US Special Forces were furious when they read these accusations against Matiullah in an internal document. "This is Taliban, and nobody else!", they shouted. A Special Forces commander decided to take Matiullah with him to the Dutch Civilian Representative—he was generally not welcome to visit the Dutch camp. With Matiullah watching, the US and the Dutch ended up in a shouting match where the US yelled at the Dutch not to make allegations about Matiullah. After that, the Dutch retreated and Matiullah was able to leave the camp without further questions about the attack and the seven wounded soldiers.

The developments of the past thirteen years of conflict in Uruzgan – but also in strategically important provinces like Kandahar and Helmand – tells us that Karzai relies heavily on his own patrons, who, often with the support of the US, systematically eliminate their competition. The main cause of the failed government (or the corruption) is this very strong but destructive system of patronage.

Setting up general peace talks between the multiple opposing groups is now very difficult compared to the early, optimistic, days after the Taliban fell. Taking the situation into account, it seems that in the early days of the 'War on Terror' in Afghanistan not many troops were needed. There were old conflicts between families and tribes stemming from before the Taliban that ultimately had to be solved. Walking through the South of Afghanistan, eating in restaurants and homes of Afghans, I often wondered what the actual role was for the foreign soldiers. It reaches too far for this book, but in Uruzgan almost every fight with foreigners was related to these old personal conflicts. Actually, the foreign intervention stirred these private conflicts. From the perspective of the warlords mentioned above, the foreigners were a free gift that gave them extremely powerful tools to continue fighting their rivals.

Obviously, the current foreign intervention hasn't done enough to strengthen a new generation of local leaders who have the respect of their people and who pursue less violent means to solve conflicts. Thirteen years after the invasion, the American troops want to leave Afghanistan in 2014 and rely more on the strongmen of Karzai who manage to keep areas quiet for the short term. In 2011 the Americans and Karzai lost two of their 'pillars' in the South: Jan Mohammed and Ahmed Wali Karzai were murdered, presumably by rivals (the Taliban didn't claim the killings). The men who filled the political vacuum are 'descendants' with the same ideas. In Kandahar, Abdul Razziq became the police commander after Ahmed Wali Karzai died. Although he is not the governor, this strongman, accused of human rights abuses, is now considered the most powerful figure in southern Afghanistan. After the Dutch left in 2010, the same happened in Uruzgan, where Matiullah Khan – with the support of the US—became the police commander and in effect the most powerful figure. In 2012 Matiullah Khan took the final step in keeping their own people in power: he appointed, with the help of Hamid Karzai, his friend Amir Mohammed Akhundza as a governor. He is the brother of governor Sher Mohammed Akhundzada who was sacked by the British in 2006 because of violent and corrupt behaviour.

Karzai and a select few struggle to stay in power. But to stay alive, the 'power game' Karzai and the Americans play since 2001 sacrificed the democratic ideals the West brought with them. The patronage networks that kept Karzai and the Americans going created tremendous nepotism, a problem that fuelled the enemy and rotted away the base and fundament of the new government.

As a consequence, the current situation calls into question the Western engagement in this conflict: was it worth it the way 'we' did it? While soldiers were fighting what they thought was a frontline crowded with 'strong Taliban', soon they discovered they were wrong. The War on Terror was much more confusing than the politicians and generals back home had told them. One failed ISAF strategy followed after the other, generals sitting behind high walls, wondering more and more: are the 'bad guys' in prison or in the palace?

Acknowledgments

Of course I want to thank Hamid Karzai for taking so much of his time to explain me his story. It's been an honour to visit the palace and get more and more understanding of Afghanstan. I also want to thank Jason Amerine who inspired me to start this research on how Hamid Karzai managed to take power from the Taliban.

I especially want to thank the family in Tarin Kot who allowed me to stay with them for the field research. They took an enormous risk by taking me into their home. I was able to hold my interviews because of their hospitality and the security measures they took. This family chose the security guard who stood at the door of the *kala* every evening. The families around us also kept an eye on everything and immediately took note of unusual company. At night the family's two daughters laid their sleeping mats next to mine and thus we formed a women's room. The idea was that then neither the Taliban nor any other enemy could enter. Thanks to this family I got to know two Afghan women, two daughters, four sons, four daughters-in-law and many delightful and curious children. I used their *kota* to interview witnesses from 2001, sometimes for days, about their country, about what they think and what they experienced. Thanks to this family I could get to know the people – I had a dress made, bought a chicken for the family and celebrated New Year's Eve with them in March. This is what I wanted to do. This is what I had so many questions about. And Tarin Kot was the town I was so afraid of. Thanks to them it was possible to put aside my apprehensions and take that step. *Manana*

In many ways, this book was a partnership between me and my dear friend N, a Pashtun from the South who learned English in Taliban-time. Unfortunately N doesn't want to be mentioned in the book because of security reasons. In our years of collaboration N dug deep, and helped me with contacts in Uruzgan. Also, he thaught me much about Afghanistan. He regularly made connections that I'd missed, and knew just how to guide interview subjects through delicate topics. Many readers complimented me on my deep knowledge of the tribal society of Afghanistan. It wasn't me who was so understanding, it was N.

In Kabul I owe thanks to my two Afghan colleagues who translated interview after interview all those weeks. They called every person I wished to see, from government secretaries to messengers. Even if I didn't have the telephone number myself, they were always able to find the man through their contacts. Their enthusiasm was contagious. They were as happy as I was when we carried out a "mission impossible" yet again. Ahmad Jawad and Habib Zahori (or "Che," as he's also called), I thank you both.

I also want to thank Afghanistan experts Alex Strick

van Linschoten and Felix Kuehn for their great contributions to the English version. Also, the American journalist Anand Gopal has been an amazing colleague, and a fantastic friend who shares the same fascination for Afghanistan (his Afghanistan-book is also out: 'No Good Men Among the Living') Without the detailed comments of the excellent and generous Thomas Ruttig I would still have made so many more mistakes. Eckart Schiewek also took a lot of time to scan the manuscript and suggested improvements where it was necessary. Thank you for that Eckart. I especially want to mention Martine van Bijlert. She's an expert with a nuanced view on the reality in Afghanistan. Without her balanced knowledge it would have been impossible for me to realise this project. Afghanistan is different in so many ways—it takes time to put aside the way you are accustomed to think about such a society. Martine helped me in an extremely smart way to put on different, local glasses. My friends Leslie Knott and Nathan Hodge were always there when I needed them. Their friendship has been of a tremendous help. Also, I want to thank Margherita Stancati, Daniel Pimlott and Elliot Hannon for their help.

I want thank the Dutch publishing house De Arbeiderspers who had trust in this project while it was my first book. For the English version I am grateful to Jan Banning of Ipso Facto and their great support to get this book out in English. I also want to thanks the Dutch journalist Hans de Vreij for suggesting the topic. Without his pointer this book wouldn't have been written. During the writing process I "hibernated" for weeks, which was hard on my family and friends. I especially want to thank Anne Blanksma for his support during this long, difficult period. I also thank my family in The Netherlands. They were always supportive of what I was doing, even when I was in Afghanistan for months at a time.

I want to thank my Dutch friends Toof Brader, Mink Nijhuis, Sandra Olsthoorn, and Esther Walstra for their help in writing the story. Especially the Dutch journalist Toof Brader was an amazing friend who was always ready to help me through this difficult writing process. Any young writer would be lucky to have such an editor and friend.

List of Main Interviewees

UNITED STATES OF AMERICA

Jason Amerine, captain of the A-team of the U.S. Special Forces who supported Hamid Karzai in Uruzgan in 2001 (July 2007).

Don Bolduc, major of the C-team of the U.S. Special Forces under command of Colonel David Fox who took over the Karzai mission from Amerine (by telephone, October 13 and December 13, 2007).

James Dobbins, then-Special Representative of the American President George Bush for the Afghan Opposition and the driving force behind the new Afghan interim government. Author of *After the Taliban, Nation-Building in Afghanistan* (by telephone, July 22, 2008).

Craig Karp, then Afghanistan expert and employed as State-Department official. He supported Dobbins (by telephone, July 15, 2008).

Wendy Chamberlin, then-U.S. ambassador in Islamabad (by telephone, September 24, 2008).

Dave Smith, then military attaché with the U.S. Embassy in Islamabad (email communication, July and August, 2008).

Daoud Yakub, lobbyist for Karzai in Washington (email communication, August 16, 2008).

Sattar Sirat, king Zahir Shah's confidant in Rome, led his delegation in Bonn in 2001, was briefly presidential candidate but eventually dropped out. He currently lives in San Diego (by telephone, January 21 and June 26, 2008; unpublished interview with Sirat by journalist David Robb).

Thom Gouttiere, president of the University of Nebraska, Karzai's friend (by telephone, December 14, 2007, May 30, 2008, May 31, 2008).

Peter Tomsen, former U.S. ambassador for Afghanistan in Pakistan and Karzai's friend (by telephone, April 29, 2008).

Peter Smyth, former U.S. Ambassador for Afghanistan in Pakistan and Karzai's friend (by telephone, May 2, 2008).

Sean Naylor, journalist with *The Army Times,* author of *Not a Good Day to Die,* about Operation Anaconda in Tora Bora in Afghanistan (by telephone, December 5, 2007 and e-mail communication).

Almut Wieland-Karimi, of the German Friedrich Ebert Stiftung, who organized several conferences during the Taliban regime for the Afghan opposition (by telephone, January 9, 2008).

David Edwards, anthropologist, affiliated with Williams University and author of *Before Taliban* and *Heroes of the Age* (by telephone, June 18, 2008).

Eckhard Schieweck, former U.N. employee in western Afghanistan during the Taliban regime. Currently political affairs officer, al-Qaeda/Taliban Monitoring Team at the United Nations (by telephone, May 27, 2007).

Dan Green, in 2006 employed by the American State Department as political advisor for the American Provincial Reconstruction Team in Tarin Kot (by telephone, January 21, 2008).

Nick Mills, author of *Karzai: The failing of the American Intervention and the Struggle for Afghanistan*, 2007, (email June 2, 2008)

ISRAEL

Tim McGirk, journalist with *Time magazine* and present in Quetta after September 11, 2001 (by telephone, May 18, 2008).

ENGLAND

Francesc Vendrell, then special U.N. envoy in Afghanistan and after September 11 involved in forming the new interim government (London, June 27, 2008).

Lyse Doucet, special reporter for BBC World, was in Afghanistan during the Russian invasion and met with Karzai. She also spoke with him after September 11, 2001 (London, June 30, 2008).

Daoud Azimi, Director of BBC Pashtu (London, July 1, 2008).

Antonio Giustozzi, Afghanistan expert at the London

School of Economics, author of various scientific papers and author of *Koran, Kalashnikov and Laptop* (by telephone, May 30 and June 4, 2006).

Robert Cooper, special envoy for former British prime minister Blair for the Afghan Opposition in 2001 (by telephone, June 3, 2008).

GERMANY

Bernt Glatzer, anthropologist and expert on Afghanistan (e-mail communication, December 4, 2007).

Citha Maass, Afghanistan expert at the Stiftung Wissenschaft und Politik (German Institute for International and Security Affairs), and involved in the country since the nineties (Berlin, January 12 and 13, 2008).

Thomas Ruttig, former journalist in Afghanistan, U.N. employee in Afghanistan during the Taliban regime and involved in 2001 as U.N. employee for the Bonn process (Oranienburg, January 11, 2008).

PAKISTAN

Kathy Gannon, journalist for press agency AP in Islamabad during September 11, 2001 (by telephone, June 19, 2008).

Rahimullah Yusufzai, freelance journalist for *Time magazine* and the BBC and authority on Pakistan and the Taliban (by telephone, July 8, 2008).

Ahmed Rashid, author of *Taliban* and *Descent into Chaos*, Hamid Karzai's friend (by telephone, August 6, 2007; London, June 30, 2008).

THE NETHERLANDS

Willem Vogelsang, former journalist in Afghanistan during the Soviet invasion, author of *Geschiedenis van Afghanistan* (History of Afghanistan), employed at the University of Leiden (Leiden, August 8, 2007).

Martine van Bijlert, Afghanistan analyst, co-director of the Afghanistan Analysts Network, stationed in Kabul (Kabul, April 2, 2008; Maastricht, June 29, 2008; Amsterdam, December 18, 2008).

Hans de Vreij, Peace and Security specialist at the Wereldomroep (World Radio).

ITALY

Enrico de Maio, Italian ambassador in Islamabad and present during the Bonn process (by telephone, June 18 and 28, 2008).

Guido Rampoldi, journalist for *La Repubblica*, present in Quetta in the weeks after September 11, 2001 (by telephone, August 28, 2008).

AFGHANISTAN

Hamid Karzai, president of Afghanistan (Kabul, February 27, March 8, August 10, 2008).

Ahmad Wali Karzai, the president's half-brother, during the Taliban regime owner of a development organisation in Kandahar city. For a long time head of the Provincial Council of Kandahar but murdered in 2011 in Kandahar.

Qayyum Karzai, Karzai's brother, then living in the U.S.

and involved in opposition activities against the Taliban, was present in Bonn (not a member of the Rome delegation, but appointed as advisor), was a member of parliament and is believed to be running for presidency in the 2014 election.

Jamil Karzai, the president's cousin, lived in Quetta during the Taliban regime and currently in parliament (Kabul, August 4, 2008).

Burhanuddin Rabbani, still officially president of Afghanistan in 2001 for the Northern Alliance, then in parliament and then leader of the biggest opposition group against Karzai, the National Front. In 2009 he became the leader of the Peace Council but was killed in 2011. (Kabul, April 2, 2008).

Yunus Qanuni, former minister of internal affairs. In 2001 for the Northern Alliance and also chairman of the U.N. meeting in Bonn (Kabul, March 1 and August 3, 2008).

Dr Abdullah Abdullah, former minister of foreign affairs for the Northern Alliance in 2001, now opposition leader (Kabul, March 2, 2008).

Amin Wardak, former army commander, involved from Pakistan in the opposition activities against the Taliban, pro monarchy and currently minister of defense (Kabul, March 2, 2008).

Amin Arsala, former minister of foreign affairs under Rabbani, then involved in the Rome process of the king and currently special advisor to president Karzai (Kabul, March 17 and April 2, 2008).

Zalmay Rasul, Chief of Staff for king Zahir Shah in Rome during the Taliban regime, participated in the Bonn conference and then became minister of aviation and security advisor for Karzai. Now minister of Foreign Affairs. (Kabul, March 6, 2008).

Pir Sayid Ahmad Gilani, prominent Afghan religious leader from the east, one of the leaders of the seven mujahedeen fighting forces against the Soviets, opponent of the Taliban, currently heads the political party National Islamic Front (Kabul, March 15, 2008).

Din Mohammed, brother of the murdered Abdul Haq, lived in Pakistan during the Taliban regime, was mayor of Kabul until 2009 (Kabul, March 13, 2008).

Mir Ahmed Joyenda, worked for the Afghanistan Research and Evaluation Unit in Kabul during the Taliban regime, and became a parliamentarian afterwards. Since a year he is back with the Afghanistan Research and Evaluation Unit. Visited Uruzgan during the Taliban regime (Kabul, November 5, 2008).

Sher Mohammed Akhundzada, lived in Quetta during the Taliban regime, worked with Karzai on opposition activities and was appointed governor of Helmand province end of 2001 (Kabul, March 7, 2008).

Kalimullah Naqibi, son of Mullah Naqibullah who negotiated peace between Hamid Karzai and the Taliban in December 2001. Naqibullah died, but his son was present on some occasions, (Kandahar, October 28, 2013).

Youssef Pashtun, engineer, lived in Quetta during the

Taliban regime, then Gul Agha Sherzai's deputy and involved in Karzai's work. Joined Gul Agha Sherzai at the end of November 2001 to Kandahar to liberate the city together with the Americans. Currently minister of development (Kabul, March 11, 2008).

Hashem Watanwal, parliamentarian for Uruzgan, lived in Sweden during the Taliban regime and was murdered in 2011, together with Jan Mohammed Khan (Kabul, November 6, 2008).

Khairo Jan, first mayor of Tarin Kot during the Taliban regime, first mayor of Tarin Kot during the Karzai regime and involved in the uprising. Then Senator for Uruzgan. Murdered in 2012. (Kabul, February 20, 2008).

Mullah Abdul Salam Rocketi, army leader during the Taliban regime, received amnesty from Karzai but was still detained by the Americans and became parliamentarian after he got released. (Kabul, August 10, 2008).

Wakil Ahmad Mutawakil, minister of foreign affairs during the Taliban regime and is currently trying to be an intermediary for the Taliban and the Afghan government (Kabul, November 11, 2007).

Mullah Zaeef, then-Taliban ambassador in Pakistan and is currently attempting to negotiate with the Taliban on behalf of the Afghan government (Kabul, February 26, 2008).

Mullah Zahir, ex-Taliban commander with Mullah Dadullah, currently unemployed (Kabul, February 20 and 25, 2008).

Abdul Hakim Munib, deputy minister during the Taliban regime, and governor of Uruzgan in 2006 and 2007. Presently member of the Pakistan-Afghanistan Jirga (Kabul, February 18, 2008).

Ashraf Ghani, worked for the World Bank during the Taliban regime, participated for the United Nations at the Bonn conference and was minister of finance for Karzai (Kabul, August 6, 2008).

Haroun Mir, lobbyist for the Northern Alliance in the United States, currently director of SIG & Partners in Kabul (Kabul, April 1, 2008).

Mohammad Wais Khetab, Pajhwok Press Agency Kabul (Kabul, November 12, 2007).

Talatbek Masadykov, worked for the U.N. mission in Afghanistan (UNAMA) during the Soviet invasion and the Taliban regime, currently Chief Political Affairs UNAMA (Kabul, August 3, 2008).

Bayazid Atsak, worked for Médecins Sans Frontières in Tarin Kot (until 1998)) (Kabul, February 17, 2008).

Nur Ul-Haq Ulumi, former communist, at present in parliament for Kandahar (Kabul, February 21, 2008).

Pacha Khan Zadran, opposition of the Taliban, from Paktia. Was present at Bonn. Became governor of this region under Karzai and parliamentarian (Kabul, March 31, 2008).

Haji Mund, a.k.a. the "Quiet One," Karzai's security guard during the Taliban regime, worked with the uprising (Kandahar, April 4, 2008; by telephone, August 7,

2008).

Mohammed Shah, worked as security guard and a kind of secretary for Karzai during the Taliban regime, worked on the uprising and is currently head of security of Karzai's residence (Kabul, March 2 and 28, 2008).

Haji Hafizullah, Karzai's security guard during the Taliban regime, worked on the uprising and is currently first secretary at the Afghan Embassy in Abu Dhabi (by telephone, August 7, 2008).

URUZGAN

Jan Mohammed, governor before the Taliban rose to power; governor of Uruzgan during the Karzai regime, until 2006. Murdered in 2011 (Kabul, March 31 and August 4, 2008).

Mualim Rahmatullah, well-known Popolzai and for a long time provincial education minister in Uruzgan until 2010 (Kabul, November 6, 2008; Tarin Kot, March 23, 2008).

Aziz Sahibzada (Aziz Agha Pir Jan), former police chief of Uruzgan for the Taliban and briefly agriculture minister for the province after the Taliban regime (March 6 and 7, 2008).

Hashem Khan, prominent Ghilzai leader from northern Tarin Kot, supported Karzai's uprising and left Uruzgan after disagreements. Murdered in 2010. (by telephone, August 9, 2008).

Abdul Ahad, from Deh Rawud, Babozai who lost many relatives in Friendly Fire incident in Shah Wali Kot

(Kabul, April 6, 2008).

Abdul Ghani Mama, Popolzai elder in Uruzgan, tower of strength for Karzai, was briefly police chief of Deh Rawud in 2007. Presently unemployed (Tarin Kot, April 20 and 21, 2008).

Farouk, Abdul Ghani Mama's brother, helped the Uruzgan uprising (Tarin Kot, April 20 and 22, 2008).

Abdul Rahim Akhundzada, major religious leader from northern Tarin Kot, Popolzai and tower of strength for Karzai (Tarin Kot, April 21, 2008).

Rozi Khan, influential Barakzai leader from Uruzgan, worked as police chief until 2006, then briefly as district governor of Chora. He died in October 2008 (Kabul, February 15, 22 and 25, 2008).

Sayid Rahim, entrepreneur from northern Tarin Kot, was Karzai's messenger in 2001 (Tarin Kot, April 21 and 22, 2008).

Mahmed Jan, judge in Uruzgan and involved in the uprising (Tarin Kot, March 22, 2008).

Tor Mawlawi, judge during the Taliban regime and became head of Provincial Council of Uruzgan (Tarin Kot, April 21, 2008).

Wali Jan, Alikozai leader from northern Tarin Kot, worked for the Afghan Red Cross and is currently unemployed. Supported Karzai during the uprising (Tarin Kot, April 20, 2008).

Haji Bahadur ("The Hero"), well-known Popolzai from Deh Rawud, loyal to Karzai, was briefly district governor and currently heads a police station in Deh Rawud but has caused much division in the town (Kandahar, April 6, 2008).

Mohammed Lal (Alikozai), prominent Alikozai leader from Durji. Worked with Karzai during the uprising and then received a district in Helmand. Currently unemployed (Kabul, November 6, 2007; February 13, 2008).

General Qader Haideri (Alikozai) was in opposition during the Taliban regime, comes from Deh Rawud and supported Karzai during his uprising. Currently has a top position with the secret service (10th Department) in Kabul (Kabul, March 1 and 6; August 28, 2008, October 20, 2013).

Ibrahim Akhundzada, renowned Popolzai leader from Deh Rawud, supported Karzai during his uprising (Kabul, August 9, 2008).

Ismael Khalili, major Hazara leader from Uruzgan, currently in parliament. He supported Karzai in 2001 (Kabul, August 8, 2008).

Sultan Mohammed (Barakzai), was police chief for the Taliban, worked with Karzai against the Taliban and supported Karzai during the expedition (Kabul, August 8, 2008).

Notes

1. Description of the weeks after 09/11 in Quetta from author interviews with Said Rahim, Tim McGirk, journalist for TIME Magazine, (visited Karzai in Quetta in the days after 09/11), Daniel Lak, journalist for BBC (visited Quetta. He was in contact with Karzai when he was in Uruzgan.), Guido Rampoldi, Italian journalist for La Repubblica, (visited Karzai in Quetta.) Ibrahim Akhundzada, tribal leader from Uruzgan, (who was invited by Hamid Karzai in Quetta). See also 'After the Taliban, Who Would Rule in Kabul?; Afghans, International Planners Ponder a Political Morass', The Washington Post, September 28, 2001.

2. Description of the Taliban-period from author interview with Evert van Bentegom and Raymond Bernardus, Dutch NGO-workers who were active during the Taliban. Bayazid Atsak, working with Médicine Sans Frontières at the time of the Taliban was questioned about the sphere in Uruzgan during the Taliban.

3. Author interview with former Taliban-minister of Foreign Affairs, Wakil Ahmed Mutawakil.

4. Edward Davids' two books give thorough insights. See also "The Importance of Tribal Structures and Pakhtunwali in Afghanistan; Their role in security and governance", Shahmahmood Miakhel, former deputy minister of Interior of Afghanistan 2003 – 2005, http://pashtoonkhwa.com/files/articles/Miakhel%20-%20Importance%20of%20Tribal%20Structures%20in%20Afghanistan.pdf.

5. Description of Karzai's rebellion during the Taliban-period from

author interviews with Hamid Karzai, Ahmed Wali Karzai, Aziz Sahibzada, Qayoom Karzai, Zalmay Rassoul, Jan Mohammed Khan, Ibrahim Akhundzada, Qader Haideri and journalist Ahmed Rashid. From the side of the Northern Alliance: Dr Abdullah Abdullah, professor Burhanuddin Rabbani, Younus Qanooni.

6. Description of Jan Mohammed from author interviews with family and friends, like Aziz Sahibzada and an anonymous friend of the Karzai-family in Kandahar who doesn't want to be mentioned in the book because of safety reasons. He worked for an international NGO before 2001.

7. Description of the Taliban taking over Uruzgan from author interviews with Rozi Khan, Aziz Sahibzada, Ibrahim Akhundzada, Said Rahim and Farouk.

8. Description from author interview with Ahmed Karzai, a nephew of Hamid Karzai. See also "Man killed in secret CIA prison allegedly saved Afghan president's life", Kathy Gannon and Adam Goldman, Associated Press, April 06, 2010. http://www.rawstory.com/rs/2010/04/06/man-killed-secret-cia-prison-allegedly-saved-afghan-presidents-life/

9. Author interview with American diplomat in Pakistan, Richard H. Smyth, principal officer in US Consulate in Peshawar from 1992 – 1996.

10. Author interview, Hamid Karzai. "Mullah Ghaus often came to my house, even months before 09/11."

11. Author interview, Hamid Karzai.

12. NSA Cables (Unclassified) December 1996. Document ID 168281600.

13. Rabbani always denied the accusation that he ordered the murder because he held Najibullah responsible for killing his family members when Najibullah was the head of the secret service.

14. Description from author interview with former American diplomat in Pakistan, Richard H. Smyth, principal officer in US Consulate

in Peshawar from 1992 – 1996.

15. Author interview with family-friend. See also 'How is Hamid Karzai Still Standing", New York Times, November 20, 2013.

16. Colleague, and co-director of Afghanistan Analyst Network, Thomas Ruttig discussed this with the king himself.

17. Author interview with family-friend. See also 'How is Hamid Karzai Still Standing", New York Times, November 20, 2013.

18. Author interview with family-friend. See also 'How is Hamid Karzai Still Standing", New York Times, November 20, 2013.

19. Author interview with family-friend and Qayoom Karzai.

20. Description of humiliation of the Karzai-family from author interviews with anonymous friend of Hamid Karzai, Qayoom Karzai, Ahmed Wali Karzai, Gulah Haider Hamidi. Amir Lalai (who died in 2011 of a heart attack) refused to be interviewed.

21. Interview Engineer Sayed, based in Peshawar, and member of one of the peace initiatives Abdul Ahad and Hamid Karzai were also part of.

22. According to Ambassador Richard Smyth Karzai was 'terribly disappointed' in the first president and his Jihadi leader Mojadedi who didn't prevent Rabbani to become his successor.

23. Author interview with Hamid Karzai and Ahmed Rashid. See also Ghost Wars, Steve Coll, page 287.

24. NSA Cables (Unclassified) December 1996. Document ID 168281600. Also from author interview with Ahmed Karzai who said that Pakistan also played a role: "He showed us the letter from Taliban leader that he was appointed to the UN in the US. But he was summoned by the Pakistani Foreign Affairs and they asked Karzai 'Why do you want to intervene in Afghanistan affairs?' He told them that Afghanistan is my country and you don't have the right to intervene. Taliban gave me this letter. But the Pakistani were not impressed. It doesn't matter the Taliban wants this, we

don't want you and if we don't want you then it's not going to happen. The then Taliban minister of Foreign Affairs Mullah Ghaus was with him."

25. From author interview with an Afghan who was with Ahmad Wali Karzai in these meetings. Other interviews with close associates of Mullah Omar confirmed the Amir's distrust in the family of Hamid Karzai, who he saw as a threat to his own position.

26. Interview Afghan diplomat who was also representing the Taliban in the US.

27. From author interview with Hamid Karzai and an American diplomat from the US State Department whose name is not mentioned because he is not allowed to talk to the media.

28. Description of Hamid Karzai's relation with his father from author interview with Ahmed Karzai and Gulam Haider Hamidi who visited the family regularly. See also Karzai in his Labyrinth, New York Times Magazine, Elisabeth Rubin, August 4, 2009.

29. From author interview with Hamidi who witnessed the accusations. Also a nephew of Hamid Karzai recounted the story (he prefers to remain anonymous because of the sensitivity of the issue).

30. Description of opposition activities during the Taliban from author interviews with Hamid Karzai, Aziz Sahibzada, Qayoom Karzai, Peter Tomsen and Almut Wieland – Karimi.

31. Unless his half-brother Ahmad Wali Karzai, who was living in Kandahar City, and had set up an NGO.

32. Author interviews with Hamid Karzai, Haji Bahadur, Jan Mohammed and Sher Mohammed Akhundzada.

33. Author interviews with Hamid Karzai, Jan Mohammed, Aziz Sahibzada, Younus Qanooni, Peter Tomsen, Haroun Mir and anonymous State Department-source who worked at the US embassy in Pakistan at that time and is not authorized to talk about these issues.

34. Description of uprising of Karzai and Massoud from author interviews with Aziz Agha, Hazara-leader (Khalili) from Uruzgan, Jan Mohammed and Hamid Karzai.

35. Description of US response to the Taliban and Osama bin Laden from author interviews with Hamid Karzai and anonymous source at State Department who worked at the embassy in Pakistan at that time. See also Descent into Chaos, Ahmed Rashid.

36. Author interview with Hamid Karzai and Ashraf Ghani. See also Hamid Karzai's testimony at the Senate Foreign Relations Committee, Near Eastern and Southern Affairs. Federal News Service, July 20, 2000.

37. Author interview with a high official of the Pakistan Military Intelligence (MI) in Quetta, who was – before 09/11 – meeting Hamid Karzai on a regular basis, 'sitting in Karzai's house, gossiping, and talking about Afghanistan'. "Karza approached us as well when he had problems with his visa and became PNG which means Persona Non Grata. My boss of the military intelligence in Islamabad wanted Karzai out on the request of the ISI. The ISI didn't trust Karzai any more because he was talking to everyone, from Ahmed Massoud, to people of the King, to the Americans. I told my boss to refuse the request of the ISI and send him a fax about this. I think that also prevented Hamid Karzai from being PNG."

38. Description from author interview with Ibrahim Akhundzada. Karzai confirmed the meeting with Akhundzada and the handover of the lists with names.

39. From author interview with Hamid Karzai.

40. From author interview with Ibrahim Akhundzada.

41. Dr hab. Jolanta Sierakowska-Dyndo, 'Tribalism and Afghan Political Traditions', http://www.wgsr.uw.edu.pl/pub/uploads/aps04/5Sierakowska-Dydo_Trybalism.pdf

42. Heroes of the Age, David Edwards. See also Goodhand and Sedra (2006): "Afghans on both sides of the conflict consistently subverted the bi-polar logic of their external backers; alliances in the field were constantly shifting back and forth between the mujahedin and pro-government militias. At the micro level Afghans would have family members in both the government forces and the mujahedin as part of a political risk spreading strategy."

43. Author interviews including Rozi Khan and Said Rahim.

44. See also Martine van Bijlert's essay "Unruly Commanders and Violent Power Struggles" in Giustozzi (ed.), *Decoding the New Taliban*.

45. Author interviews with inhabitants of Uruzgan, but also NGO-employees who visited Uruzgan during the Taliban, like Bayazid Atsak, and a Western employee of ICRC who was based in the hospital in Tarin Kot (and likes not to be named because of ICRC-policy).

46. Transcript: Bush Says U.S. Will Do "Whatever It Takes" to Defeat Terrorists, http://www.globalsecurity.org/military/library/news/2001/09/mil-010915-usia-01.htm.

47. Description of the first days of the war on terror in Afghanistan: Bush at war, Bob Woodward; Jawbreaker, Gary Berntsen; First In, Gary Schroen.

48. From author interview with Din Mohammed.

49. From author interviews with Peter Tomsen and Din Mohammed.

50. From author interview with Hamid Karzai. In the first interview Hamid Karzai denied the CIA's involvement. After the Uruzgan-helpers disclosed the name of the CIA agent who assisted their expedition, Karzai confirmed his relation with the agent Graig in the second interview. Then he also provided the picture of him and the agent when they were together in Tarin Kot in November 2001. Karzai confirmed visiting the CIA in Islamabad before he

entered Uruzgan but didn't want to disclose the subject of the conversation.

51. From author interview with Hamid Karzai and Ahmed Wali Karzai.

52. From author interview with high official of the Pakistan Military Intelligence (MI) in Quetta, who kept an eye on Graig's activities in the hotel. According to the official Graig also received Gul Agha Sherzai, the former governor of Kandahar, who would in December enter Afghanistan together with American Special Forces.

53. From author interview with Hamid Karzai.

54. "After the Taliban, Who Would Rule in Kabul? Afghans, International Planners Ponder a Political Morass", Washington Post, September 28, 2001.

55. From author interview with Ahmed Rashid.

56. From author interview with Guido Rampoldi.

57. Author interviews with Hamid Karzai and Mohammed Shah.

58. More about these first days can be found in 'First In', Gary Schroen.

59. Description of Hamid Karzai leaving Quetta from author interviews with Ahmed Wali Karzai, Haji Mond, Haji Faisula and Ahmed Karzai. There is confusion about the exact date Karzai left Quetta. According to Ahmed Wali Karzai and Haji Mond they left the day after the bombing started (October 7 2001). Journalist Ahmed Rashid told me Karzai left 'two or three days later'. Journalists who were in Quetta say it must have been around October 12. John Daniszewski of TIME Magazine told me: "I think I saw him there on Oct. 12 and went back in just two or three days to look for him again, and was told he had gone. Only later I did realize he had been infiltrated into Afghanistan." See also his article 'Life after Taliban is what they're planning', TIME Magazine, October 13, 2001.

60. From author interview with Haji Mund.

61. From author interview with Kalimullah Naqibi, son of Mullah Naqibullah.

62. Author interview with Ahmed Wali Karzai.

63. Author interview with high official of the Military Intelligence (MI), who asked to remain anonymous because he is not authorized to discuss these issues. He used to meet Hamid Karzai on a regular basis before 09/11.

64. About crossing the border, I interviewed Hamid Karzai, Ahmed Karzai, Haji Mund and Haji Hafizullah. Stories that Karzai entered Afghanistan by helicopter were not confirmed in my research. They seem to confuse the second time Karzai entered Afghanistan (in November). That was with a helicopter.

65. Author interview with high official of the Military Intelligence, who asked to remain anonymous because he is not authorized to discuss these issues. He used to meet Hamid Karzai on a regular basis before 09/11.

66. Description of Karzai in Kandahar from author interviews with Hamid Karzai, his nephew Ahmed Karzai, Haji Mond and Haji Faisula. Description of the phone call to Rome from author interview with the then cabinet chief or the Rome Group, Zalmay Rassoul and Hamid Karzai.

67. From Soldiers of God, Robert Kaplan.

68. Description of the payment of the satellite phones from author interview with Ahmed Wali Karzai and Said Rahim.

69. Description of the attack on Hamid Karzai from author interview with Hamid Karzai, Rozi Khan, Jan Mohammed Khan and Aziz Sahibzada.

70. Description of the supplies from author interviews with Said Rahim and Karzai's nephew Ahmed Karzai who travelled back and forth Quetta too. The description of the CIA who provides money

from author interview with Ahmed Wali Karzai.

71. From author interview with James Dobbins, Special Representative of the United States for the Afghan opposition. See also At the Center of the Storm, My Years at the CIA, George Tenet.

72. From author interview with Hamid Karzai, Aziz Sahibzada, Said Rahim and others who were present.

73. From author interviews with Abdul Ghani Mama, Aziz Sahibzada, Mohammed Lal, Mualim Rahmatullah, Said Rahim and Hamid Karzai.

74. Author interview with Mohammed Lal and his family who hosted Karzai in Durji.

75. Author interview with Ahmad Karzai and Mohammed Shah.

76. Description of weapon dropping from witnesses who were with Karzai (like Mohammed Lal, Qader Haideri and Farouk), and Hamid Karzai himself. See also Frontline, PBS (interview Hamid Karzai).

77. From author interview with witnesses like Mohammed Lal, Ibrahim Akhundzada and Hashem Watanwal. Wali Jan, who joined Hamid Karzai too, says he thinks Mullah Bahadur helped Karzai.

78. New York Times, 'Afghan trying to do 'big things' at big risk', November 5, 2001, http://www.nytimes.com/2001/11/05/world/a-nation-challenged-taliban-foe-afghan-trying-to-do-big-things-at-big-risk.html

79. Ibid.

80. From author interview with captain Jason Amerine.

81. From author interview with Karzai's assistant Qader Haideri and BBC-journalist Daoud Azimi (who was in London at that time, receiving the calls from Karzai's group).

82. Description of the scene on Karzai's promises for his people from

author interview with Ibrahim Akhundzada.

83. Description of the phone call with the CIA from author interview with Hamid Karzai.

84. From author interview with Hamid Karzai.

85. From author interviews with witnesses like Mohammed Lal and Qader Haideri.

86. From author interview with captain Jason Amerine. See also Wounded Royalist Rescued by US, The Telegraph, November 8, 2001. For Karzai trying to deny his rescue see: Southern Rebel Leader Appeals for Supplies, The Telegraph, November 12, 2001.

87. From interviews with Hamid Karzai. In the first talks Karzai denied, but after showing more evidence given by his fellow tribesmen who were with him in the helicopter, the president admitted.

88. Description of the dialogue between the CIA-agent and the Afghan from author interview with one of Karzai's helpers, Mohammed Lal.

89. From author interview with James Dobbins.

90. Description of dialogue between Dobbins and Dr Abdullah Abdullah from author interviews with both.

91. Author interview with Ambassador Wendy Chamberlin.

92. From author interview with Haji Mond, Haji Faizullah and Mohammed Lal.

93. The fourth helicopter landed on the wrong spot. After the Americans were rescued by Karzai's people, they joined the A-team again. From author interview with Jason Amerine, Haji Bahadur and Hamid Karzai.

94. One helicopter landed on the wrong location and Haji Bahadur and his Afghans have to search for hours before they find the lost Special Forces.

95. From author interview with Hamid Karzai and Jason Amerine.

96. Description of the infiltration of the C-team into Afghanistan from author interview with Donald Bolduc.

97. Scene in kala in Tarin Kot from author interviews with Jon Bolduc.

98. From author interview with Francesc Vendrell, Deputy Special Representative of the United Nations for Afghanistan.

99. From author interview with Peter Neuss, manager of the hotel.

100. From Descent into Chaos, Ahmed Rashid.

101. From author interview with Francesc Vendrell who was Special Representative for the United Nations during the Taliban.

102. From author interview with Francesc Vendrell, James Dobbins, Sattar Sirat and Ashraf Ghani (who was with Brahimi on the UN team).

103. From author interview with Francesc Vendrell who was in Kabul at that time.

104. From author interviews with Sattar Sirat and Amin Arsala.

105. From author interview with Hamid Karzai.

106. From author interview with Italian ambassador in Pakistan, Enrico de Maio (present at the Bonn Conference).

107. From author interview with Hamid Karzai and Zalmay Rassoul. At that time Rassoul called Karzai about the rumour.

108. Sphere conference from author visit to the hotel, interviews with personnel in the hotel, James Dobbins, Vendrell, representatives from the Northern Alliance and others.

109. Author interview Younus Qanooni.

110. Description of response of the Rome Group to the telephone call from Hamid Karzai with the Bonn Conference from author interview with members like Amin Arsala, Amin Wardak, Sattar Sirat

and Thomas Ruttig who attended the meeting as a member of the United Nations delegation.

111. From author interview Ahmed Wali Karzai.

112. From author interview with Sher Mohammed Akhundzada.

113. Description of the Taliban looking for a way out from Descent into Chaos, Ahmed Rashid.

114. Description of the surrender of Dadullah from author interview Hashem Khan, Ahmed Wali Karzai and Said Rahim.

115. Description from author interview with Hamid Karzai and Haji Mund who made the plans in Jacobabad.

116. From author interview with Hamid Karzai, Aziz Sahibzada and Haji Bahadur.

117. Author interview with Qayyum Karzai.

118. Author interview with Abdullah Abdullah.

119. Author interview with Qanuni and Vendrell.

120. author interview with cabinet chief Zalmay Rassoul.

121. Author interview with Hamid Karzai and the then president Burhanuddin Rabbani.

122. Author interview, Hamid Karzai, and author interview with Kalimullah, the son of Mullah Naqibullah. Mullah Naqibullah died in 2007. Kalimullah was in charge of the satellite phones and walkie-talkies during Karzai's uprising and was with his father most of the time, he said.

123. Description of Karzai in Said Kalim Alay from author interview with Haji Bahadur.

124. Author interview with Don Bolduc.

125. See also 'Report: Air controller called in friendly fire', The Boston Herald, March 27, 2002.

126. From Descent into Chaos, Ahmed Rashid.

127. From author interview with Hamid Karzai and Lyse Doucet.

128. Description of the meeting about surrender of the Taliban from author interview with Mullah Rocketi.

129. Author interview with Kalimullah, the son of Mullah Naqibullah. Both were present at the meeting.

130. Kalimullah says that Karzai first didn't get permission from the US to see the Taliban. After a while, Naqibullah and Karzai convinced the US to go ahead with the surrender and trust Karzai on dealing with the Taliban.

131. Kalimullah wasn't with his father at the time, so the account of Naqibullah isn't included.

132. From author interviews with participants in the Taliban – meeting.

133. From author interview with Abdul Rahim Akhundzada.

134. Chayes, Sarah, The Punishment of Virtue, page 60.

135. Chayes, Sarah, the Punishment of Virtue, Author interview son Kalimullah.

136. Chayes, page 60.

137. Observation of Don Bolduc, from an author interview.

138. 'The Battle for Afghanistan', Anand Gopal, New America Foundation, November 2009.

139. The New York Times, December 19, 2009. Afghan Killing Bares a Family Feud, http://www.nytimes.com/2009/12/20/world/asia/20karzai.html?pa gewanted=all&_r=0

140. Dailymail, March, 10, 2011, 'NATO forces 'mistakenly' kill cous of Afghan President Hamid Karzai during raid on house' http://www.dailymail.co.uk/news/article-1364913/NATO-special-forces-kill-cousin-Afghan-President-Hamid-Karzai-house-raid.html

CPSIA information can be obtained at www.ICGtesting.com
Printed in the USA
LVOW07s2125221214

420048LV00005B/315/P